PROFILES

ONE EVENT SIX BIOS

FREEDOM HEROINES

By Frieda Wishinsky

Susan B. Anthony

Elizabeth Cady Stanton

Jane Addams

Ida B. Wells

Alice Paul

Rosa Parks

SCHOLASTIC INC.

Photo Research: Dwayne Howard

Photo credits

Cover: *Anthony*: Everett Collection Inc./Alamy; *Stanton*: ibid; *Addams*: ibid; *Wells*: University of Chicago; *Paul*: Everett Collection Inc./Alamy; *Parks*: Photos 12/Alamy

Page 6: Everett Collection Inc./Alamy; page 7: Library of Congress; page 9: Susan B. Anthony Museum & House; page 10: ibid; page 12: Library of Congress; page 13: The Granger Collection; page 14: National Archives; page 15: Library of Congress; page 17: ibid; page 18: ibid; page 19: Bettmann/Corbis; page 20: Library of Congress; page 22: ibid; page 23: National Archives; page 24: Corbis; page 25: Washington Post/Getty Images; page 26: Everett Collection Inc./Alamy; page 30: Library of Congress; page 31: Corbis; page 32: Library of Congress; page 33: ibid; page 34: The Granger Collection; page 35: Susan B. Anthony Museum & House; page 36: Library of Congress; page 37: The Granger Collection; page 38 (both): ibid; page 39: Library of Congress; page 40: Bettmann/Corbis; page 42: ibid; page 44: Library of Congress; page 45: ibid; page 46: The Granger Collection; page 48: Everett Collection Inc./Alamy; page 49 (both): University of Illinois at Chicago; page 50: Library of Congress; page 53: The Imageworks; page 54: Chris Lawrence/Alamy; page 55: The Granger Collection; page 56: Wallace Kirkland/Photo Researchers, Inc.; page 57: North Wind Picture Archives/Alamy; page 58: Getty Images; page 59: The Granger Collection; page 60: Culver Pictures, Inc./SuperStock; page 61: University of Illinois at Chicago; page 62: ibid; page 63: Corbis; 65: University of Illinois at Chicago; page 66: ibid; page 68: University of Chicago; page 69: Everett Collection Inc./Alamy; page 70: The Granger Collection; page 72: Birch Harms/Getty Images; page 74: University of Chicago; page 75: The Granger Collection; page 77: Corbis; page 78: Library of Congress; page 79: Alamy; page 80: Library of Congress; page 81 (both): University of Chicago; page 82: Library of Congress; page 83 top: ibid, bottom: The Granger Collection; page 84: University of Chicago; page 86: Everett Collection Inc./Alamy; page 88: Alamy; page 89: Everett Collection Inc./Alamy; page 90: Mary Evans Picture Library/Alamy; page 91: Mary Evans Picture Library/The Image Works; page 92: Hulton-Deutsch Collection/Corbis; page 93: UK History/Alamy; page 94: Library of Congress; page 95: The Granger Collection; page 97: Bettmann/Corbis; page 98: ibid; page 99: Getty Images; page 100: Bettmann/Corbis; page 101: ibid; page 102: Mary Evans Picture Library/Alamy; page 104: The Granger Collection; page 105: Associated Press; page 106: Bettmann/Corbis; page 107: ibid; page 108: Photos 12/Alamy; page 110: Library of Congress; page 112: Time & Life Pictures/Getty Images; page 114: akg-images/Newscom; page 116: NY Daily News/Getty Images; page 117: Time & Life Pictures/Getty Images; page 118: Bob Adelman/Corbis; page 119: Bettmann/Corbis; page 120: Newscom; page 121: Time & Life Pictures/Getty Images; page 122: World History Archive/Newscom; page 124: Time & Life Pictures/Getty Images; page 125: Bob Adelman/Corbis; page 126: The Granger Collection; page 127: Time & Life Pictures/Getty Images; page 128: AFP/Getty Images.

ISBN 978-0-545-42518-6

10 9 8 7 6 5 4 3 2 1 12 13 14 15 16

Printed in the U.S.A. 40
First edition, December 2012
Designed by Kay Petronio

CONTENTS

SUSAN B. ANTHONY

"We shall some day be heeded, and . . . everybody will think it was always so . . . They have no idea of how every single inch of ground that she stands upon today has been gained by the hard work of some little handful of women in the past."

SUSAN B. ANTHONY was a pioneering advocate for women's rights. She worked tirelessly, often with her friend Elizabeth Cady Stanton, to change attitudes and laws in the United States so that women would be treated equally and fairly, and granted the right to vote.

EARLY YEARS

Susan Brownwell Anthony was born on February 15, 1820, on a farm in Adams, Massachusetts. She was the second child in her family. Her family believed in the **Quaker** faith, which opposes all war, encourages people to live a simple life, and stands up for the equality of men and women. Anthony's grandfather had fought in the American Revolution and served in the Massachusetts legislature.

From the time she was little, Anthony was surrounded by women who worked for a living. She and her siblings were expected to pitch in to help with chores on the farm. When she was six, the family moved to a large brick house in Battenville, New York, where her father ran cotton mills. He also educated his children and the women who worked in his mills. Later, he hired experienced women to teach them at their homes.

Anthony herself began to teach in local schools when she was fifteen. Even then, she felt it was unfair that she was paid less than male teachers for the same work. When she turned seventeen, she attended

Anthony's family home in Battenville

stories of how they both had been shunned by organizations they had help organize and support—just because they were women.

Anthony told Stanton how she had worked to organize a temperance convention. But when she asked to speak in front of the convention, instead of being welcomed, the male chairman said, "The sisters were not invited to speak but to listen and learn." Anthony was furious. How could they treat women this way? They'd contributed as much as men to the movement. They had a right to be heard, too. Anthony was so angry, she stormed out of the meeting. A few women joined her, but many stayed in their seats, worried that if they spoke up, men would call them "meddlesome" and "disturbers."

Stanton told Anthony that when she'd asked to speak in front of the World Anti-Slavery Convention, she'd been denied the right, too—just because she was a woman.

Susan B. Anthony as a young woman

The friends decided that if men in the temperance movement wouldn't treat women with respect, they'd start their own temperance organization. In April 1852, Susan B. Anthony, Elizabeth

Stanton, and five hundred women met in Rochester, New York, to establish the Women's State Temperance Society. Stanton even wrote a speech insisting that if a woman had an alcoholic husband, she should have the right to divorce him.

FIGHTING FOR RIGHTS

That September, Anthony attended her first women's rights convention in Syracuse, New York, and was appointed secretary. She pushed for women to be admitted to college and advocated that they refuse to pay taxes unless they could own property and leave churches that didn't treat them equally. The local newspapers scoffed at Stanton and Anthony and their demands for equal rights. They called them "frantic and contemptible." But the newspapermen's narrow-minded attitude only strengthened Anthony's determination to speak up. She was now convinced that women had to be granted the vote. Without it, they'd never have the power to change their lives.

For the next few years, Anthony traveled from town to town, organizing meetings, gathering petitions, and speaking up. The press continued to mock her ideas, but what really stung was that even women in the temperance movement refused to support her position on equality.

Both men and women mocked Anthony and Stanton

The drunkard's progress: from the first glass to the grave

when they wore Amelia Bloomer's short dresses. Although the **bloomers** made walking easier and more comfortable, Anthony and Stanton realized that wearing the outfits was getting in the way of their message about equal rights for women. The friends decided they had to return to wearing their tight-fitting, long dresses. As Anthony said, "The attention of my audience was fixed upon my clothes instead of my words."

In 1855, Anthony traveled to every county in New York State, speaking, petitioning, and promoting the cause of equal rights. She used her own money to travel and often had to sleep in unheated rooms. Most of her talks were well-attended. Some people came to hear her speak out of curiosity. Others believed in her cause. Even a few newspapermen, who disagreed with her positions, were impressed with her determination and straightforward talk. One journalist wrote: “We cheerfully accord to her credit as a public speaker . . . expressing herself with clearness and many times with elegance and force.”

A woman wearing bloomers in the 1800s

Despite hardships and the physical pain of speaking for hours and traveling for days, Anthony was convinced that her efforts were critical to all women. Everywhere she went, she saw evidence of women who had suffered because they had few rights and no control even over their own money and property. The executive committee chairman of the American antislavery movement was so impressed with her energy, persistence, and organizational skills, he asked her to arrange speaking tours not just for herself but for others, too. It was a welcomed way to make money, and Anthony said yes.

Although Anthony appreciated the support, many women, like Stanton, were married with children and couldn't devote all their time to women's rights. Anthony was disappointed that her friends had families and other concerns. She felt marriage was a "defection" to the cause. She believed that fighting for women's rights should come ahead of anything else.

Anthony realized that Stanton had seven children and a busy household to run. She knew it was getting more difficult for her to balance her family duties and writing speeches, so Anthony pitched in and helped. After all, Stanton was her friend and a gifted writer and speaker. Anthony wanted to make sure she had time to do both.

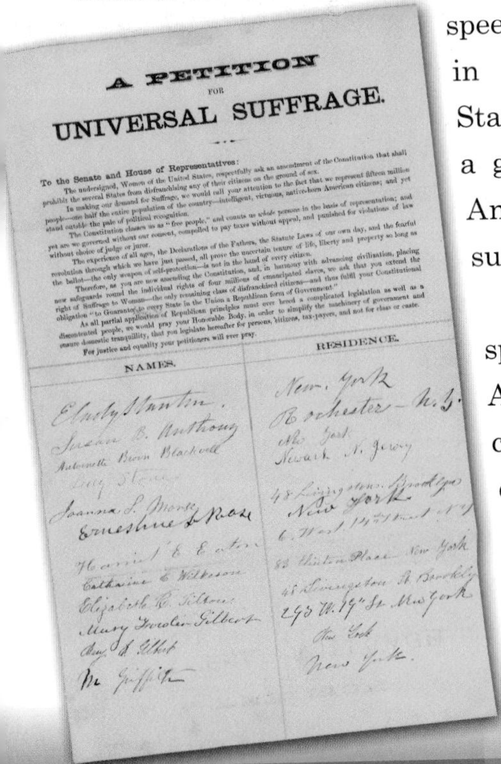

A PETITION FOR UNIVERSAL SUFFRAGE.

To the Senate and House of Representatives:

The undersigned, Women of the United States, respectfully ask an amendment of the Constitution that shall prohibit the several States from disfranchising any of their citizens on the ground of sex.

In making our demand for Suffrage, we would call your attention to the fact that we represent fifteen million people—one half the entire population of the country—intelligent, virtuous, native-born American citizens; and yet stand outside the pale of political recognition.

The Constitution classes us as "free people," and counts us *whole* persons in the basis of representation; and yet are we governed without our consent, compelled to pay taxes without appeal, and punished for violations of law without choice of judge or juror.

The experience of all ages, the Declarations of the Fathers, the Statute Laws of our own day, and the fearful revolution through which we have just passed, all prove the uncertain tenure of life, liberty and property so long as the ballot—the only weapon of self-protection—is not in the hand of every citizen.

Therefore, as you are now amending the Constitution, and, in harmony with advancing civilization, placing new safeguards round the individual rights of four millions of emancipated slaves, we ask that you extend the right of Suffrage to Woman—the only remaining class of disfranchised citizens—and thus fulfill your Constitutional obligation "to Guarantee to every State in the Union a Republican form of Government."

As all partial application of Republican principles must ever breed a complicated legislation as well as a discontented people, we would pray your Honorable Body, in order to simplify the machinery of government and ensure domestic tranquillity, that you legislate hereafter for persons, citizens, tax-payers, and not for class or caste.

For justice and equality your petitioners will ever pray.

NAMES.	RESIDENCE.
Elizabeth Cady Stanton	New York
Susan B. Anthony	Rochester—N.Y.
Antoinette Brown Blackwell	New York
Lucy Stone	Newark N. Jersey
Joanna S. Morse	48 Livingston St. Brooklyn
Ernestine L. Rose	New York
Harriet E. Eaton	6. West 14th Street N.Y.
Catharine C. Wilkeson	83 Clinton Place New York
Elizabeth R. Tilton	48 Livingston St. Brooklyn
Mary Fowler Gilbert	293 W. 19th St. New York
Mary E. Gilbert	New York
M. Griffith	New York

Stanton was a riveting speaker, but Stanton's and Anthony's views were often considered too radical, even within the women's rights movement. In 1859, Stanton spoke up at the National Women's Rights Convention, pushing not

A crowd of women joining the National Woman Suffrage Association in 1869

just for equal rights and opportunities, but promoting her proposal that a woman should be free to divorce an alcoholic husband as well. The audience was shocked and disapproving. Many didn't want to deal with divorce-law reform. But Anthony agreed with her friend. It was important to change marriage and divorce laws if women were going to have any degree of equality. Anthony said that in marriage "man gains all—woman loses all."

CHANGE AND THE CIVIL WAR

On the eve of the Civil War in 1861, many who'd fought for equal rights for women changed their focus to fight for freedom for slaves. That year, although Anthony worked

George Francis Train

magazine. Anthony and Stanton called it *The Revolution*, but many of their friends in the women's rights movement found some of the ideas they advocated for to be too radical.

But when Anthony and Stanton refused to support the Fifteenth Amendment granting blacks the vote because it ignored women, there was even more controversy and greater dissension. Anthony and Stanton stuck by their position. They felt it wasn't fair to only grant men the vote. Why were women completely left out? Anthony and Stanton traveled out west campaigning against the ratification of the Fifteenth Amendment. Instead, they supported a Sixteenth Amendment, which would give women the vote, too. Many people came to hear them but few agreed with their views.

ON THEIR OWN

Anthony and Stanton were battling against the views of old supporters and long-standing friends. Disappointed that their ideas were not being heard, they founded a new organization, the National Woman Suffrage Association.

National Woman Suffrage Association meeting in the 1870s

They decided that men would not be allowed to participate in their group.

By the spring of 1870, *The Revolution*, no longer funded by George Francis Train, was going under. Anthony had poured her life's savings into keeping the magazine afloat and now she had little money left. She'd spent so much she was almost bankrupt. Stanton was growing weary of all the fighting within the women's movement and stopped attending most of the meetings. Instead she took off on a speaking tour. She wanted to make enough money to send her daughters to college. Anthony felt hurt, alone, and isolated.

But soon after, the friends traveled together from Illinois to California to give talks. For a while, all was

1873 *Daily Graphic* cartoon of a masculine Susan B. Anthony campaigning for equality

judge in Albany, New York, refused her request and fined her $1,000. Anthony refused to pay and announced that she'd rather go to jail. Her attorney was so dismayed, he put up the bail money for her. He said, "I could not see a lady I respected put in jail."

Anthony was out of jail, but she still had to face a trial. Before her case was set to go to court in June, she crossed the county speaking about her experiences. She asked, "Is it a crime for a citizen of the United States to vote?"

The trial, which took place on June 17, was stacked against Anthony from the beginning. The judge wanted to please his political cronies and wrote his opinion before a single piece of evidence was presented. He refused Anthony's request to testify for herself, stating that women were incompetent to testify and told the jury to find her guilty. When he asked Anthony if she had anything to say, she said, "You have trampled under foot every vital principle of our government." The judge then tried to stop

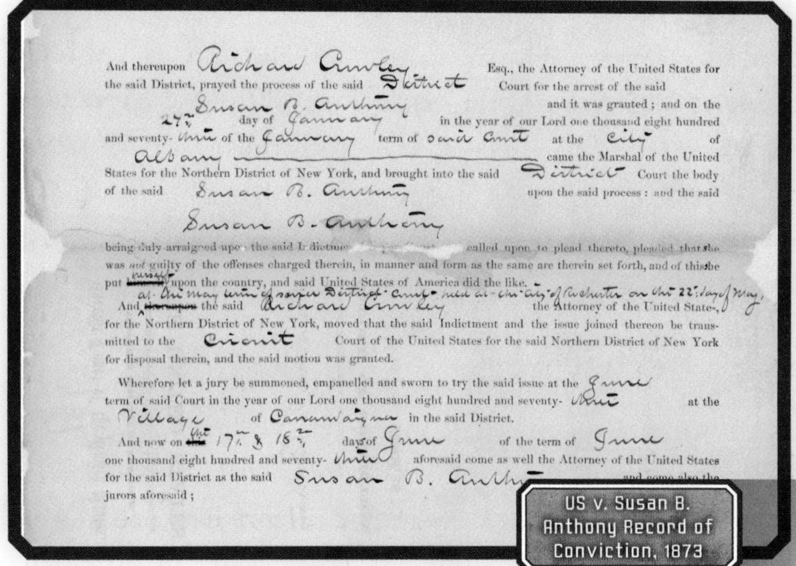

And thereupon Richard Crowley Esq., the Attorney of the United States for the said District, prayed the process of the said District Court for the arrest of the said Susan B. Anthony and it was granted; and on the 24th day of January in the year of our Lord one thousand eight hundred and seventy-three of the January term of said Court at the City of Albany came the Marshal of the United States for the Northern District of New York, and brought into the said District Court the body of the said Susan B. Anthony upon the said process: and the said Susan B. Anthony being duly arraigned upon the said Indictment [illegible] called upon to plead thereto, pleaded that she was *not* guilty of the offenses charged therein, in manner and form as the same are therein set forth, and of this she put herself upon the country, and said United States of America did the like.

And at the May term of said District Court held at the City of Rochester on the 22d day of May, the said Richard Crowley the Attorney of the United States, for the Northern District of New York, moved that the said Indictment and the issue joined thereon be transmitted to the Circuit Court of the United States for the said Northern District of New York for disposal therein, and the said motion was granted.

Wherefore let a jury be summoned, empanelled and sworn to try the said issue at the June term of said Court in the year of our Lord one thousand eight hundred and seventy-three at the Village of Canandaigua in the said District.

And now on the 17th & 18th days of June of the term of June one thousand eight hundred and seventy-three aforesaid come as well the Attorney of the United States for the said District as the said Susan B. Anthony and come also the jurors aforesaid;

US v. Susan B. Anthony Record of Conviction, 1873

her from publicly saying anything more, but Anthony kept speaking out. She was outraged that women continued to be denied the basic right to vote.

Then she made sure that three thousand copies of her court transcript were distributed around the county. Although she was convinced that it would probably be impossible, at least in the near future, for women to be granted the vote through the United States courts, she was determined to keep stating the case. She wanted the public to keep thinking about women's rights. She refused to pay the $100 fine the judge imposed. No further legal action was taken against her.

LATER YEARS

For the following ten years, Anthony, Stanton, and Matilda Joslyn Gage wrote the six-volume *History of Woman Suffrage*. It was painful to recall all that the friends had suffered to advance women's rights. Anthony wrote: "It makes me sad and tired to . . . see the terrible strain I was under every minute then, have been since, am now and shall be for the rest of my life."

But despite advancing age and worsening health, Anthony never stopped working for women's rights. The right to vote was the most important issue to her. She made sure that the National Woman Suffrage Association held its annual meetings in Washington, D.C., where the politicians

Members of the first International Council of Women, including Susan B. Anthony and Elizabeth Cady Stanton

lived and worked. She continued to petition. She took every opportunity to remind the public and politicians about women's rights. She was persistent and passionate. She became a familiar figure in Washington, D.C., wearing her dark outfit brightened by a red shawl.

Sculpture of Anthony and Stanton in the Capitol Rotunda in Washington, D.C.

In 1888, she founded the International Council of Women, broadening the push for women's rights to other countries. She tirelessly raised funds for women to be admitted to the University of Rochester in 1900. She believed that "failure was impossible."

Susan B. Anthony died in 1906 of heart failure. At the time of her death, four western states—Wyoming, Colorado, Idaho, and Utah—had granted women the vote.

The Nineteenth Amendment granting women the right to vote in all of the United States was finally ratified in 1920.

ELIZABETH CADY STANTON

"Woman will always be dependant until she holds a purse of her own."

ELIZABETH CADY STANTON was a writer and speaker who fiercely championed women's rights. She helped write the *Declaration of Sentiments*. Modeled after the Declaration of Independence, it stated that women deserved to be treated fairly and equally.

EARLY YEARS

Elizabeth Cady was born on November 12, 1815, in Johnstown, New York. From the time she was little, she was feisty and determined. Her father was a prominent judge, and Lizzie, as she was called, was the middle child in the family. Stanton adored her father, but he doted on the boys in the family, especially Stanton's brother Eleazar. Her father often said, "Oh, my daughter, I wish you were a boy."

Stanton longed to impress her father and prove that she was smart and capable, too. When Eleazar was killed in a carriage accident, Stanton was even more resolved to make her father proud of her. She decided to study Greek. Mastering that difficult language would surely prove to her father that she was as accomplished as any boy!

Stanton approached the pastor of their church, Dr. Hosack, and begged him to teach her Greek. Dr. Hosack agreed and several times a week, Stanton studied with him. Soon she was able to read the exercises in her Greek grammar book. Although her father was pleased when Dr. Hosack told him how she'd excelled, he still said, "Oh, my daughter, I wish you were a boy."

Stanton was discouraged, but she wouldn't give up. At Dr. Hosack's suggestion, her father sent her to the Johnstown Academy, where her brother Eleazar had attended. Stanton

During the short ceremony, Elizabeth refused to say the word *obey*, which was traditional in the service. Even Henry was startled by how strongly she felt. But she was resolved. She believed that she and Henry were equals, and she had no intention of obeying anyone.

A NEW LIFE

Stanton loved the trip across the Atlantic to England. She loved the sea. She liked to read and play chess and imagine what London would be like. When the ship docked, she was surprised at how dark and gloomy London first appeared, but she was excited to meet new people, especially Lucretia Mott, a women's rights advocate. She and Mott had a lot in common. Many of the antislavery conference participants were opposed to women taking an active role in the discussions and debates. Women were only permitted to observe the events. Even Henry agreed with this position. But Mott agreed with Elizabeth. It wasn't fair. They were all fighting for rights for slaves, but men were denying women the same rights. Women had a right to speak their minds, too.

Lucretia Mott

After their year in England, the Stantons moved back to the United States, where Henry started a law practice. By 1845, Elizabeth had given birth to three boys. She enjoyed her growing family, entertaining, and meeting new people in Boston, but it was a struggle, too. Henry wasn't making enough money to pay the bills. Elizabeth's father offered them a house in Seneca Falls, New York, to help out with expenses. Although she wasn't thrilled about living in the country, far from everyone she knew, the family relocated.

Stanton and her daughter Harriot

Henry *was* happy about the change. He could travel around the country speaking against slavery, take care of his legal business, and further his political ambitions. But Elizabeth was stuck at home with her growing family.

Although Henry sent her books, newspapers, and pamphlets, and she became friends with the local postmistress, Amelia Bloomer, who shared many of her views, it wasn't enough. In 1848, Elizabeth was delighted

The Stantons' house in Seneca Falls

to hear from her friend Lucretia Mott, who invited her to a meeting about women's rights at Jane Hunt's home in nearby Waterloo, New York. It was a meeting that would change everything.

CONVENTIONS AND BLOOMERS

All the women at Jane Hunt's house were Quakers, except Stanton. She was also the youngest of the group. The women at the meeting were determined to push forward change and ensure that women were granted equal rights. They decided to hold a women's rights convention at the Wesleyan Chapel in Seneca Falls only five days later, on July 19 and 20. They drew up a declaration of women's rights and listed women's grievances on divorce laws, owning property, lack of equality in education, work opportunities, and the right to vote. At the end of the two-day convention one hundred people signed the declaration.

Newspapers not only criticized but also mocked the women's rights convention. They scoffed that women wanted change, fairness, and the right to vote. The general reaction was so negative and intense that some of the women who'd signed the declaration withdrew their names. Stanton didn't. She only grew more determined to work toward equal rights and the right to vote. During this time, her friend Amelia Bloomer decided to begin a small magazine, *The Lily*, and Stanton wrote articles for it.

Soon other reformers, like Lucy Stone, joined them, and more meetings and conventions were held in support of women's rights. Stanton couldn't attend most of them because of her growing family. In 1851, Stanton gave birth to a fourth boy.

THE FIRST CONVENTION

EVER CALLED TO DISCUSS THE

Civil and Political Rights of Women,

SENECA FALLS, N. Y., JULY 19, 20, 1848.

WOMAN'S RIGHTS CONVENTION.

A Convention to discuss the social, civil, and religious condition and rights of woman will be held in the Wesleyan Chapel, at Seneca Falls, N. Y., on Wednesday and Thursday, the 19th and 20th of July current; commencing at 10 o'clock A. M. During the first day the meeting will be exclusively for women, who are earnestly invited to attend. The public generally are invited to be present on the second day, when Lucretia Mott, of Philadelphia, and other ladies and gentlemen, will address the Convention.*

* This call was published in the *Seneca County Courier*, July 14, 1848, without any signatures. The movers of this Convention, who drafted the call, the declaration and resolutions were Elizabeth Cady Stanton, Lucretia Mott, Martha C. Wright, Mary Ann McClintock, and Jane C. Hunt.

That same year, when Stanton's cousin Libby Smith arrived for a visit wearing long trousers topped by a short dress, Stanton was charmed. What a great idea! Stanton and Amelia Bloomer copied Smith's outfit, and Bloomer drew a pattern and printed it in her magazine. The outfit became known as *bloomers* and caused a storm of comments. But Stanton loved wearing bloomers. It was easy to walk around in them. You didn't trip on stairs the way you would in a long skirt. Bloomers made perfect sense.

A woman wearing bloomers in the 1800s

A LIFE-CHANGING FRIEND

After two years of being teased and even harassed about wearing bloomers, Stanton reluctantly decided she had to stop wearing them and go back to long skirts. It wasn't that she was going to give up her battle for women's rights. It was just that the controversy over bloomers was getting too much attention. And after meeting Susan B. Anthony, a young teacher from Rochester, New York, who was visiting Amelia Bloomer, Stanton was even more determined to forge ahead with her battle for women's rights.

Amelia Bloomer

The two women became close friends and allies, and each had different talents. Anthony was excellent at organizing and planning. Stanton was terrific at writing and speaking. Anthony had become active in the temperance movement, which railed against heavy drinking and the negative way it affected families. The friends now decided they'd use their talents, energy, and drive to push not just for temperance but also for equal rights and opportunities for women. Anthony even helped Stanton with her growing family. Between raising young children and trying to control her rambunctious older boys, Stanton needed help. Anthony helped her find Amelia Willard, a caring woman who helped run Stanton's busy and active household.

With the added help at home, Stanton and Anthony

decided to take a bold step. They'd speak to the men running New York. They'd travel to Albany, the capital, and present their case for women's rights in person. The friends gathered petitions. They wrote a speech that Stanton would deliver. The big question was, how would she be received by a roomful of men in Albany?

STANTON SPEAKS OUT

It was uncomfortable standing in front of a hall filled with male politicians, but Stanton spoke with authority and

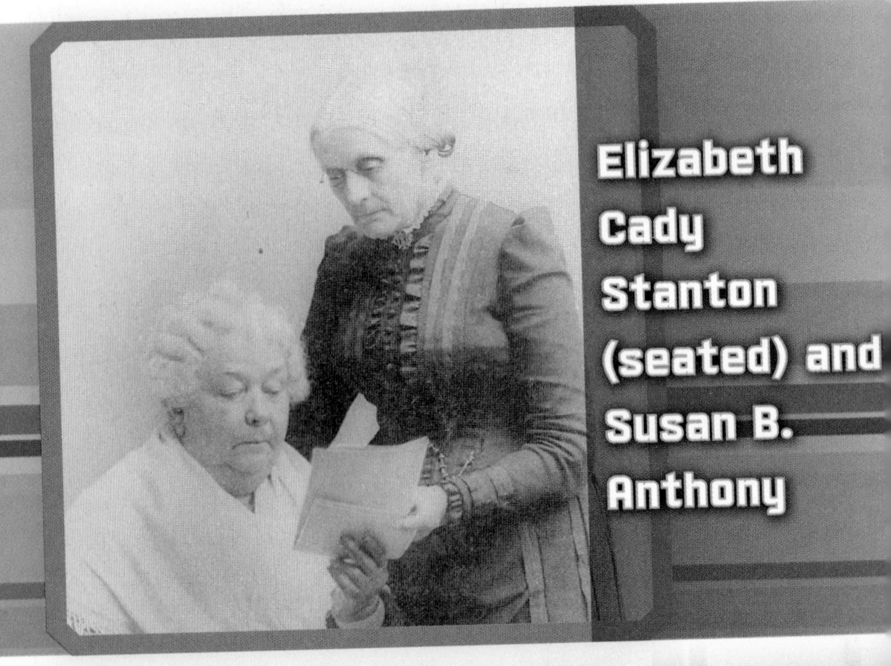

Elizabeth Cady Stanton (seated) and Susan B. Anthony

Men opposing women's suffrage

conviction. She was treated politely, but the next day, the politicians and the newspapers hurled criticisms at her. It was clear that the rights Anthony and Stanton were fighting for were not going to come quickly or easily. And to complicate matters more, Stanton's family was still growing. By 1859, she gave birth to her seventh child. She was older now, and it took her a longer time to recover from the birth.

Advertisement for the book *Uncle Tom's Cabin*

That year, there was increased tension in the United States. The country was deeply divided over slavery. The 1852 publication of Harriet Beecher Stowe's book *Uncle Tom's Cabin* continued to cause a great stir. John Brown, a militant abolitionist, wanted to arm slaves, and he and his followers seized an arsenal at Harpers Ferry, Virginia (now West Virginia). His capture, arrest, and hanging added fuel to the division in the United States.

John Brown

Stanton's father also died that year. Although he had often vowed to disinherit her because of all her political activity, in the end, he didn't. Instead, he left Stanton money, which gave her more freedom, as did her mother's help with her children. But now with all the turmoil, the struggle for women's rights was going to have to wait while the country dealt with the threat of a civil war.

THE CIVIL WAR

On November 6, 1860, Abraham Lincoln was elected president of the United States. In December of that year, the southern states, which opposed Lincoln's antislavery views, seceded from the Union. Stanton and Anthony were caught up in abolitionist work. They held meetings and handed out petitions. Henry had a job in the customs house in New York City, and the family had to move from Seneca Falls. Anthony came up to help pack the family's belongings.

On April 12, 1861, the Civil War began when the Confederates opened fire on Fort Sumter, South Carolina. Anthony, a **pacifist**, was against all war, but Stanton believed that this war was justified. They were both disappointed that it took President Lincoln until

HARPER'S WEEKLY.
A JOURNAL OF CIVILIZATION.
NEW YORK, SATURDAY, FEBRUARY 18, 1865.

Scene in the House of Congress to amend the Constitution, January 31, 1865

January 1, 1863, to issue the Emancipation Proclamation, which gave most slaves their freedom. Abolitionists like Stanton and Anthony wanted an amendment that gave all slaves their freedom. That finally happened in 1865, when the Thirteenth Amendment was passed.

Stanton and Anthony rejoiced, but they were also disappointed. Why didn't the Thirteenth Amendment give any additional rights to women, too? They knew that few people in government or at the newspapers agreed with their position. Women's rights continued to be discounted and bypassed.

Stanton addressing the first Women's Rights Convention in Seneca Falls on June 20, 1848

When the war was over, Stanton decided to stand as an independent candidate for Congress from the eighth district of New York. Even if she couldn't vote, men could vote for her! Out of almost twenty-three thousand votes, Elizabeth only won twenty-four. She was soundly defeated but she'd also made her point.

A SPLIT IN THE MOVEMENT

When the first national convention of the women's rights movement was held in 1869, there was a split in how the participants saw the direction and goals of the movement. Some opposed Stanton's and Anthony's positions and formed a group called the American Woman Suffrage Association. It was headed by Lucy Stone of Boston and admitted men and women to meetings. Stanton and Anthony started a group called the National Woman Suffrage Association, and they only allowed women to attend their meetings.

As the women's rights movement gained greater recognition, Stanton was invited to speak around the country. She was excited about the opportunity to travel, talk about her beliefs, and also make money to help send her daughters to college. Finally, there were a few colleges that admitted women!

HEADING WEST

At first, Stanton and Anthony traveled west together to push for women's suffrage. Their first destination was Kansas. The state was considering two amendments to its constitution, and one was for women's suffrage.

Traveling mainly by train and stagecoach, the friends headed out on bumpy and often dangerous roads, but that didn't stop them. Stanton spoke everywhere—in log cabins, schools, barns, and churches. Sometimes the women traveled by night. Sometimes they traveled in the rain and tramped through mud. But the worst part of the trip was the bedbugs. It was almost impossible to sleep in a bed filled with insects that made you squirm and itch all night. Despite all the hardships, Stanton loved speaking out for women's rights.

But the message ran into an unexpected roadblock. Some men worried that if women were granted the vote, they'd encourage temperance, limiting access to alcoholic beverages. Many men were opposed to that! When the vote was counted, Kansas voted against the women's suffrage amendment.

Caricature of Elizabeth Cady Stanton

Stanton wasn't discouraged, especially when George Francis Train offered to help. His money financed a magazine. Stanton and Anthony called it *The Revolution*, and Stanton loved organizing and writing. Not everyone in the women's rights movement approved of the militant tone of the magazine, and certainly not its name. They thought Stanton's views were too extreme. And then Train was jailed in Ireland for unlawful political activities. The money dried up and the magazine soon folded.

But Stanton kept traveling despite bad weather, uncomfortable accommodations, and unpleasant food. In 1872, she described the trip to her sister:

> "Monday I rode in an open wagon across the prairies, spoke that evening and the next morning, and in the afternoon rode the same distance back again. Then I took the car to Hastings, arrived there at eleven o'clock and as there was an exciting murder trial on, I could not get a place to sleep. So with my clothes all on I laid on a broken-down old lounge . . ."

Her trips were full of ever-changing and exhausting episodes like these, but she kept going. Her resilience, outgoing personality, and friendly spirit charmed everyone. She traveled and spoke for twelve years. But by the time she was in her sixties, she'd had enough. It was time to give up touring across the country.

WRITING ABOUT IT

When Stanton finally stopped her grueling speaking schedule, she turned to writing. With Anthony's help, she put together papers, diaries, notes, speeches, and letters. After four years of working together, they, along with Matilda Joslyn Gage, produced six thick volumes of material and called their project the *History of Woman Suffrage*. They sent their completed books to libraries around the country, happy that they had recorded the history of the early suffrage movement in the United States for future generations.

Now that Stanton was nearing seventy, she also reveled in her expanding family and enjoyed traveling to visit some of her children and grandchildren who'd moved to France and England. While she was visiting England, she heard that her husband had died at the age of eighty-two. Although they had lived apart for many years, the news of his death was still a shock.

Elizabeth Cady Stanton

As the years passed, Stanton was pleased that women had made *some* advances. In many states, they

Susan B. Anthony and Elizabeth Cady Stanton, lifelong colleagues and friends

could own property and manage their own money. There were colleges that accepted women. Women began to study law and medicine. But women still could not vote, and they still weren't paid the same salary as men for the same work. But Stanton didn't give up hope. In the Wyoming territory, women were given the right to vote, and when Wyoming became the forty-fourth state in the Union, it continued to grant women full political rights. Despite her advancing age, Stanton kept on advocating for women's rights and speaking at the National Woman Suffrage Association's annual convention.

Elizabeth Cady Stanton, 1815-1902

On her eightieth birthday, her friends rented the Metropolitan Opera House in New York City and threw her a big party celebrating her life and achievements. And even as she grew frailer and her eyesight began to fail, she kept reading, writing, and pushing for women's rights. Her last letter was to President Theodore Roosevelt, encouraging him to go down in history as a supporter of an amendment granting women the vote.

Elizabeth Cady Stanton died in her sleep on October 26, 1902, at the age of eighty-seven.

JANE ADDAMS

JANE ADDAMS worked to end child labor, supported women's and worker's rights, helped people in poverty, and encouraged respect for all cultures. She established Hull-House, the nation's first settlement house, to aid those in need. In 1931, Addams became the first woman to win the Nobel Peace Prize.

EARLY YEARS

Jane Addams was born on September 6, 1860. She was the youngest child in a family of nine children. Her family's roots went back to William Penn, who founded the colony that became Pennsylvania. The family had Quaker roots and followed Quaker beliefs in working hard, respecting the rights of all people, and opposing war.

Jane Addams as a young girl

Addams's mother died when she was two. Her sisters took care of her and often spoke about their mother and her strong beliefs and teachings. Addams's father was a wealthy businessman, bank owner, and state legislator. He was a friend of President Abraham Lincoln. Addams adored her father and always wanted to make him proud of her.

John H. Addams, Jane's father

When Addams was six and on a trip to Freeport, Illinois, with her father, they passed streets with broken-down, crowded houses. It was Addams's first encounter with people living in poverty. It made a

Jane Addams as a young woman

big impression on her. She told her father, "When I am a grown woman I am going to buy a big house. Then the poor children can come and play in my yard whenever they want." Little did she know how her early words would one day come true.

Addams was always an avid reader. Her house was filled with books, and her father encouraged her to read. She loved Charles Dickens, William Shakespeare, and essays by Ralph Waldo Emerson when she was older. All these books influenced the way she saw the world.

GROWING UP

When Addams was eight, her father married Anna Haldeman. It was hard to adjust to a new stepmother. Addams didn't like her stepmother's rules and often avoided her so they wouldn't get into arguments. She missed her father's constant attention, but she liked her new stepbrother, George, who was close to her in age and became her playmate.

Although people thought Addams was pretty, she was self-conscious about a back problem. It made her bend over when she walked, and she felt it made her look ugly and crippled.

Addams was self-disciplined from the time she was young and would wake up early to read and study. She was a good student and liked helping other students. When she grew up, Addams was eager to attend Smith College, one of the few schools to offer women a bachelor's degree. But her father was opposed and sent her instead to the Rockford Female Seminary. Addams excelled at Rockford. She rose to the top of her class, was voted class president, and became head of the literary society, editor of the school newspaper, and valedictorian of her graduating class of 1882.

Addams didn't want her studies to stop there. She applied to medical school—a radical decision for a woman of her time. Her parents were again opposed. They believed that the main role of a woman was to get married and have children. They thought that becoming a doctor would get in the way of her finding a husband. But Addams was determined to attend medical school, despite their disapproval.

In 1881, Addams's father unexpectedly died. She was devastated and lost all interest in her medical studies. To make matters worse, she was experiencing terrible back pain. One physician told her that she wouldn't live a year in her condition. Addams had painful surgery and for six months after was flat on her back. She was also forced to wear an uncomfortable, heavy brace for a year.

After she recovered, she traveled to Europe. Wealthy young women of the day often toured Europe with family or friends to learn about art and culture. Addams toured with her stepmother and a few friends. She marveled at all the sights and enjoyed visiting the museums and sitting at cafés. But she was appalled at the poverty she saw in cities like London. The horrible conditions that poor families endured were heartbreaking, and Addams was stunned by how many wealthy people she met who ignored the plight of the poor.

Addams toured Europe for two years, and when she returned home, she didn't know what to do next with her life. She was distraught that she had no purpose or goals. She'd always felt that she would do something to make a positive change in the world, and now she was twenty-seven years old and she hadn't accomplished anything yet.

A JOURNEY AND A PURPOSE

Although she was still unsure of her direction, Addams decided to travel to Europe again. Luckily, she'd inherited enough money from her father so she could afford to travel.

Drawing of a London scene of poverty

This time she'd travel with a former classmate, Ellen Starr. The friends shared a love of literature and art, but they had different temperaments. Starr was lively and expressive of her feelings. Addams was even-tempered and steady.

When the two women landed in Madrid, they attended a bullfight. Starr was horrified by the bloody, brutal show she witnessed in the ring and left. Addams stayed and was stunned to discover that she enjoyed the event. Later that day, she was horrified by her reaction. How could she sit there and watch creatures being killed so brutally and not do anything? It made her aware of how much needless suffering there was in the world. It made her realize she wanted to do something to help people—not just travel around the world. She shared her feelings with Starr, and

Toynbee Hall, London

her friend was eager to help people in need, too. So when Addams visited Toynbee Hall in London a month later and met university students who were helping the poor by providing places for them to live, it gave her an idea. She and Starr would start a similar **settlement house** back home in Chicago.

HULL-HOUSE

When Addams returned to Chicago, she and Starr looked for a place they could turn into a settlement house similar to Toynbee Hall. The house in Chicago had to be big; easy to reach; and in the middle of a poor, multicultural neighborhood. In 1889, they found a house at the corner of Polk and Halsted that they thought would work. It had been built as a country house for Charles Hull in 1856. It was a sprawling two-story redbrick mansion that stood between a saloon and a funeral parlor. Some people believed it was haunted.

Addams's and Starr's aim was to create a place of acceptance, comfort, continuing education, and help with basic needs. Addams believed that everyone in society would benefit when the poor had better lives and access to education so they could find good jobs—not just menial, low-paying work. She wrote: "The good we seek for ourselves is precarious and uncertain until it is secure for all of us." Helen Culver, who had inherited the house, allowed them to use all of it for their settlement house and offered it to them rent-free.

Hull-House, Chicago

Some of the members of Addams's family, especially her stepmother, were shocked by her involvement with Hull-House and her plans to live among the poor. They felt it wasn't proper for an unmarried woman of her class to live this way. Even those who supported her goals thought she'd probably never succeed. Despite the opposition and the huge task of cleaning up the neglected old house, Addams and Starr persisted.

But it wasn't just Addams's relatives who were unenthusiastic about Hull-House. At first, many of the local people were skeptical about these two wealthy young women who'd moved into the neighborhood. Small boys threw stones at the house. Some people thought that Addams and Starr were missionaries who wanted to convert them to a different religion.

Addams with children in Hull-House

Slowly, curiosity drew people into Hull-House. And when they came, many embraced the settlement house. Working mothers were happy that there was a safe place to leave their small children while they worked. Older children liked the social clubs and

Children cared for in the Hull-House day nursery in Chicago, 1890s

art classes. The hungry found a place where they could purchase good food cheaply. Addams and Starr were delighted that Hull-House was becoming a vital center in the neighborhood. They were also amazed at the generosity of so many, who although poor themselves, came to the aid of a neighbor or friend who experienced illness, death, or hard times.

For the first few years, Addams poured her own money into Hull-House. Addams and Starr worked tirelessly, organizing classes, keeping the house in shape, and fund-raising for Hull-House. Addams also used her contacts among the wealthy in Chicago to raise funds. She soon realized that it made sense to delegate her daily work at Hull-House so she could spend more time raising money.

Hull-House Choir, 1910

She knew that raising money was crucial to keep programs running at Hull-House. Addams's own fortune was dwindling.

PART OF THE COMMUNITY

Within a few years of opening, Hull-House became an integral part of the community called the Nineteenth Ward of Chicago. The neighborhood was mostly made up of Jewish, German, Greek, and Italian immigrants. The settlement house offered classes in literature, English, music, and drama. It also provided a variety of clubs, a gym, a coffee house, and a library. Eventually twenty-five women would reside at Hull-House.

A few years after opening Hull-House, Addams realized that although the house provided vital services to the community, it was equally essential to change laws that made poor people's lives difficult. Soon, Addams began to speak up publicly against **sweatshops**, where people worked long hours in terrible conditions for little pay, and the widespread use of child labor. She also advocated for better city services in poor areas.

Addams helped organize the Congress of Social Settlements held at Hull-House. In her talks, she insisted that not only conditions but also laws that affected the poor had to be changed. By 1892, her speeches received national attention, and more people became aware of the work that settlement houses were doing in communities around the United States. When the Chicago World's Fair brought thousands of people to the city in 1893, many came to visit Hull-House, and its fame grew even greater. There were soon nineteen more settlement houses around the United States, mostly in big cities like Boston, New York, Philadelphia, and Chicago. Hull-House was the largest. It had expanded to three buildings and now included an

Chicago World's Fair poster, 1893

Unemployment line, circa 1890

art gallery, which was a gift from a trustee. In only four years, Hull-House had blossomed from an idea into a well-known and respected organization.

TOUGH TIMES

That summer, there was a severe economic depression in the United States, and many people in the Nineteenth Ward lost their jobs. It was terrible to see so many people unemployed. People had already made little money and often lived paycheck to paycheck, but the economic downturn made conditions worse. Times were tough and so many people were unemployed that some people felt hopeless and even ashamed that they couldn't find work. Addams used much of her energy and time to help the unemployed.

But it wasn't just Addams and Starr who worked at Hull-House. It attracted young women, often from well-to-do homes, who were eager to change conditions. They believed that the best way to help the poor and unemployed was through action, and many got their start working at Hull-House. Alice Hamilton, who was trained as a doctor and in 1919 was the first woman appointed to the faculty of Harvard University, worked in industrial medicine, where she tried to improve conditions in factories. Louise deKoven Bowen worked to establish the nation's first juvenile court so that young people weren't tried as adults. Florence Kelley threw her energy into changing the miserable conditions in sweatshops.

Six years after opening Hull-House, Addams took on an additional and essential job: She became the garbage inspector for the Nineteenth Ward. She knew how crucial it was for people to live in a clean environment. She wanted to help people stay as healthy as they could, despite living in crowded, unsanitary buildings.

Jane Addams

In her new role, Addams rose at dawn to make sure that the wagons hauled away the garbage properly and on time. She recognized that it was easy to get sick, especially when you lived in dirt-filled streets, were overworked, and didn't have the proper nutrition. Addams felt that her job was to prevent that from happening in the best way she could. That message hit home especially hard when Addams herself came down with typhoid fever.

CHALLENGES

Addams's doctor insisted she rest and regain her strength. A colleague from Hull-House took over her garbage inspector duties. When Addams recovered, she took time off and traveled abroad. It was an exciting trip. She was thrilled to meet the famous writer and humanitarian Leo Tolstoy in Russia, although she felt uncomfortable when he chided her for wearing fashionable clothes. He also told her that the important thing in life was to live simply and work hard.

Fourteen hundred men and women paid tribute to Addams at a dinner given in Chicago on January 20, 1927

When she returned to Chicago, Addams tried to follow Tolstoy's example and do more chores around Hull-House. She soon realized that her most effective role was to speak out against injustice and to stand up to politicians like Johnny Powers from the Nineteenth Ward, who tried to buy people's votes. She also continued to give talks about helping the poor and reforming unjust laws against women, children, and workers. Her speeches were often mentioned in the press, and Jane Addams became famous around the world.

In 1898, as Addams was about to give a lecture in Iowa, a U.S. ship called the *Maine* was sunk in Havana, Cuba. Americans were outraged at the way Spain treated the citizens of its colony Cuba. Spain was blamed (unfairly it turned out) for sinking the *Maine*. That anger led to

Jane Addams at an anti-war rally in 1915

war with Spain and eventually war over control of the Philippines, which Spain also occupied. Addams spoke up against the war. Many disagreed with her.

After meeting black reformer and writer Ida B. Wells, Addams also spoke out against **lynching**—the horrible practice, mainly in the South, of brutally killing black people unjustly accused of crimes. Although Wells was glad that Addams opposed lynching, Wells strongly disagreed with the way Addams presented the facts. Wells claimed the issue was not just that lynching was brutal, but also that the men were innocent.

Addams ran into more controversy when she stood up for treating everyone fairly, including **anarchists**, a group who didn't believe in the rule of government. Addams stood by her position, even after an anarchist shot President William McKinley in 1901. Despite the angry comments she received from people claiming she was sympathetic to the anarchist point of view, Addams saw it simply as an issue of fairness.

BOOKS AND HONORS

In 1902, Addams published her first book, *Democracy and Social Ethics*. She continued to lobby and speak up against child labor and helped pass laws prohibiting children under the age of fourteen from working. Some states had laws on the books against child labor, but many were not enforced. In the South, children as young as five often worked in mills.

Collage of Jane Addams's life

In 1905, she was appointed to the Chicago school board. In 1907, she published another book, *Newer Ideals of Peace*, and became more involved in the movement for women's rights. In 1909, she helped found the **NAACP**, the National Association for the Advancement of Colored People. In 1910, she received the first honorary degree ever granted to a woman by Yale University. That same year, she published her autobiography, *Twenty Years at Hull-House*. The book became a bestseller.

WORLD WAR I

In 1914, the assassination of Austrian Archduke Ferdinand by a Serbian sparked World War I. Long-simmering land disputes and rivalries inflamed the leaders of Europe, and soon Germany, Austro-Hungary, and eventually Turkey

were at war against the Allies, which included Britain, France, and Russia. It was a war that started with dreams of glory but was fought in long, drawn-out battles with heavy losses on all sides.

Addams, who didn't believe in any war, opposed World War I. Her views evoked sharp criticism. Despite the harsh comments, Addams helped Secretary of Commerce Herbert Hoover provide food for America's European allies at the end of the war in 1918. But when she traveled to Berlin in 1919, the suffering of the starving children in Germany stunned her. Even though the Allies had fought the Germans in the war, Addams believed now was the time to help their former enemies recover. Many disagreed with her, and she was again criticized again for her opinions.

But that didn't stop Addams. In 1919, she became president of the Women's International League for Peace and Freedom. Over the next ten years, Addams continued promoting peace and equal rights for all. In 1920, the Nineteenth Amendment to the constitution was finally ratified, granting women the right to vote. In 1926, Addams suffered a heart attack and her health began to fail, but she continued writing about her life, her work, and her views.

In 1931, Jane Addams was awarded the Nobel Peace Prize, making her the first woman given the honor. The same year she had surgery for a tumor.

Jane Addams died on May 21, 1935, of cancer.

IDA B. WELLS

"Brave men do not gather by thousands to torture and murder a single individual, so gagged and bound he cannot make even feeble resistance or defense."

IDA B. WELLS was a teacher, speaker, and writer who fearlessly wrote about lynching—the horrific way some blacks were killed by whites in the South after the Civil War. She was also active in the women's suffrage movement and worked toward ensuring that men and women of all races were treated fairly and equally.

EARLY YEARS

Ida B. Wells was born a slave in Holly Spring, Mississippi, in 1862. By the time she was three, the Civil War was over and all slaves were emancipated. Wells's mother, Elizabeth, had grown up a slave. She'd been cruelly separated from her family and sold from one plantation to the next. Her father, James, was the son of a black slave and a white plantation owner. Although he had a privileged position on the plantation and was taught carpentry, he was still considered a slave. He knew that even with **emancipation**, there would be a fight to be treated fairly and have equal access to educational and economic opportunities.

Wells's parents valued education and sent Wells, the eldest, and her siblings to a school run by a white northern Methodist. Wells was taught to read and write and encouraged to work hard and have good manners. Her mother was strict. She made sure her children did their homework and finished their chores.

Woodcut of Wells in 1891

Wells's parents spoke about their lives before emancipation and about how things were changing in the new, post–Civil War era called Reconstruction. Some of the change was frightening. Some in the southern

A freeman, John Campbell, vainly begs for mercy from the KKK in Moore County, North Carolina, August 10, 1871

white communities were angry and resentful that they'd lost the war and disliked the new way of life they felt had been imposed on them. Some even joined the **Ku Klux Klan**, a secretive white organization that harassed and terrorized people who didn't agree with their views. The Klan accused many black people of crimes and often lynched them before they could be brought to court or trial. The violent activities of the Ku Klux Klan left many blacks worried and fearful for their lives. No one knew where the Klan might strike next.

Despite living in fear, James Wells attended political meetings. His group discussed ways for blacks to have greater economic opportunities and live safer lives.

YELLOW FEVER

Luckily, Wells and her family didn't experience the Klan's brutality directly. Wells went to school, studied, did her chores, visited her grandparents, and helped her family.

But when she was sixteen and visiting her grandmother Peggy in Memphis, Tennessee, she heard terrible news: Yellow fever had hit her community. The disease killed her parents and one of her brothers.

Wells was devastated. How could she go home? What if she caught yellow fever, too? Everyone warned her not to return. Even passenger trains wouldn't stop in Holly Springs because people feared they'd catch yellow fever. Little was known about how the disease was spread in those days. (We now know it's spread by infected mosquitoes.)

But Wells was determined. Her surviving siblings needed her. She hopped on a freight train and arrived home to a town of deserted streets. Many in the community had died. Two of her siblings were sick. Wells was grateful that the local doctor, Dr. Gray, a kind white man, helped her family. Dr. Gray spoke warmly of her father and his efforts to help the community when yellow fever first struck.

When the epidemic finally died down, friends of Wells's family decided that her brothers and sister should be split up among different families and that one of her siblings, Eugenia, who was paralyzed, should be sent to a poor house. Wells said she could take care of them all. Her father had left them the house and a little money. She'd find a job and keep the family together.

Wells took a teaching test, and when she passed, she found a teaching position six miles away from home. During the week, Wells's grandma Peggy, who moved to Holly Springs to help out, looked after the smaller children. When Grandma Peggy had a stroke, a family friend helped out. On the weekends Wells came home, did the laundry, cooked, and cleaned. It was a burden for such a young woman, but Wells did what she had to do to keep her family together.

MEMPHIS

When Wells was nineteen, she knew she needed a change. She also wanted to earn more money, so she decided to move to Memphis to find a better-paying teaching job. Her siblings were now older, and two of her aunts offered to board them. Memphis was a bustling city with factories, a waterfront, and railways. Blacks had built churches and schools. They could ride the same bus as whites, vote, and serve in public office.

Memphis Reservoir, Tennessee

When Wells found a job outside of Memphis in a country school in Woodstock, she rode the train to work and studied for her licensing exam so she could teach in the city.

One day on the train, as usual, she sat down in the seats reserved for "ladies" in first class. But this time, the conductor demanded that she move to a car in the back of the train—the one for smokers and blacks. Wells refused. She'd paid for her seat. She was entitled to sit there! The conductor grabbed her by the hand and tried yanking her out of her seat. As soon as he touched her, Wells bit his hand. The stunned conductor stormed off for help and recruited three men to drag Wells out of her seat. As they pulled her, the sleeve of her linen coat ripped. Wells got off the train.

Although she had stood up for her rights, it was a humiliating and infuriating experience. Wells was so outraged that she hired a lawyer to sue the railroad. While she waited to hear back, she found a job teaching first grade in a Memphis school. Wells began to teach but realized that she didn't enjoy teaching a large, rowdy, unmotivated class. And then she heard that the black lawyer she'd hired had been paid off by the railroad to prevent the case from going to court. She was hurt and angry and hired another lawyer. When the case was finally heard, Wells was awarded $500.

SPEAKING HER MIND

Wells didn't like teaching, but she enjoyed life in Memphis. She went to picnics, church fairs, the theater, concerts, and visited friends. She even took speech lessons. She joined a lecture club and one day a member of the group offered her a job as a writer for the *Evening Star*, a newsletter. Wells enjoyed writing. After she described being dragged off the rail train, she was asked to write a weekly column for the *Living Way*, a black church publication. Her column was popular, and soon Wells was contributing to other black newspapers. Her opinions earned her both praise and criticism, but she kept writing. Conditions for blacks had become increasingly difficult in the South after Reconstruction, and Wells wrote about how the new Jim Crow laws restricted the rights of black people on trains, restaurants, streetcars, and parks. Blacks were being forced to sit separately from whites all over the South.

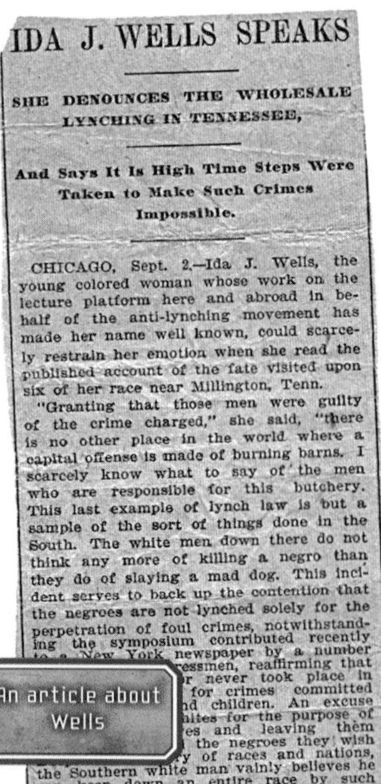

IDA J. WELLS SPEAKS

SHE DENOUNCES THE WHOLESALE LYNCHING IN TENNESSEE,

And Says It Is High Time Steps Were Taken to Make Such Crimes Impossible.

CHICAGO, Sept. 2.—Ida J. Wells, the young colored woman whose work on the lecture platform here and abroad in behalf of the anti-lynching movement has made her name well known, could scarcely restrain her emotion when she read the published account of the fate visited upon six of her race near Millington, Tenn.

"Granting that those men were guilty of the crime charged," she said, "there is no other place in the world where a capital offense is made of burning barns. I scarcely know what to say of the men who are responsible for this butchery. This last example of lynch law is but a sample of the sort of things done in the South. The white men down there do not think any more of killing a negro than they do of slaying a mad dog. This incident serves to back up the contention that the negroes are not lynched solely for the perpetration of foul crimes, notwithstanding the symposium contributed recently to a New York newspaper by a number ... [illegible] ressmen, reaffirming that ... [illegible] r never took place in ... [illegible] for crimes committed ... [illegible] nd children. An excuse ... [illegible] hites for the purpose of ... [illegible] es and leaving them ... [illegible] the negroes they wish ... [illegible] y of races and nations, the Southern white man vainly believes he can keep down an entire race by such methods of oppression and intimidation. The South has more than once insisted upon being left alone with the negro problem. The Nation has obligingly accommodated her, and to-day the spectacle is pre-

An article about Wells

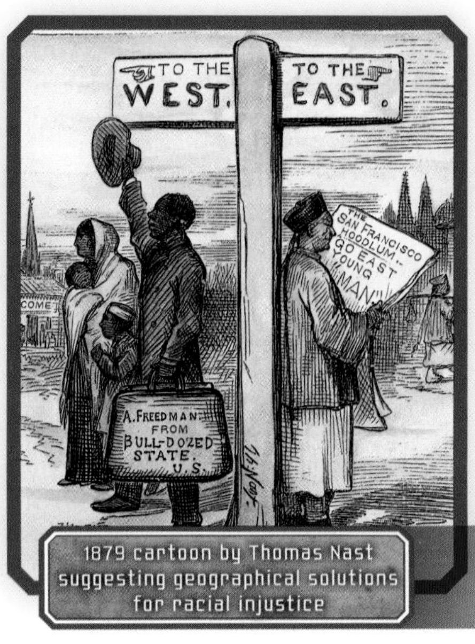

1879 cartoon by Thomas Nast suggesting geographical solutions for racial injustice

In 1887, as the atmosphere became increasingly hostile to blacks, the courts retried Wells's case against the railroad. This time the ruling went against her. The court stated that the railroad had done nothing wrong in dragging Wells out of the seat she'd paid for. The railroad didn't have to pay her a cent. Wells was charged $200. She was crushed by the new decision and the new attitude in the South.

In 1889, Wells bought a one-third interest in a black newspaper, *Free Speech and Headlight.* She continued writing articles that encouraged blacks to work hard and save money. She also criticized black schools, which were not maintained properly and hired poorly trained teachers. The Memphis school board was so enraged by Wells's opinions that they wouldn't hire her back to teach. And to Wells's disappointment, the parents of the black students at the schools didn't stand up for her, either.

IDA B. WELLS, TROUBLEMAKER

When Wells heard that T. Thomas Fortune, editor of the *New York Age*, was starting an Afro-American organization to fight against discrimination, she was thrilled. She spoke eloquently at the group's second convention in 1891. Soon, the word was out. Ida Wells was outspoken and a troublemaker.

But even more trouble was about to swirl around her. After Wells's paper published a piece supporting blacks who protested lynching by setting fire to their town in Kentucky, whites in the area were enraged, and *Free Speech and Headlight* was accused of stirring up violence. One of the paper's publishers, Reverend Taylor Nightingale, was convicted of assault and fled to Oklahoma. Wells and J. L. Fleming were now in charge of the paper. Wells wanted to drum up business for the paper, so she traveled to nearby states to promote it. While she was away, her friend Tom Moss, and his friends who owned a new grocery store in Memphis, were lynched because a white grocer resented the competition and provoked a showdown. Moss and his friends were warned that a mob was going to attack their store, so they armed themselves. In the scuffle that followed, three white men were wounded and the black grocers were arrested. Before they could go to trial, the grocers were dragged out of the city jails and shot. Wells was outraged at her friend's murder. She hurried home to comfort Moss's family.

How could this happen to a man who was just trying to run a respectable business? Wells knew Moss, and she knew he wouldn't have become involved in a fight unless he had no choice. After Moss and his friends were lynched, a mob shot at blacks, raided the grocery store, and destroyed it.

A lynch mob and their dogs

Wells had to do something. She protested by writing about the events in her newspaper. She believed that lynching was a way whites tried to frighten and control blacks. She suggested that blacks stop supporting white businesses and stop riding streetcars. She encouraged blacks to leave Memphis for good. In two months, six thousand black people followed her advice. The white community couldn't believe it. They were losing workers and business.

Meanwhile, Wells began reading more about lynching. What she read shocked her. So many people had been

19th century Front Street, Memphis

lynched. Her sharp words against lynching drew threats from the white community. In 1892, hoodlums invaded Wells's office and destroyed it.

Wells was forced to leave Memphis.

NOTHING STOPS WELLS

Wells moved to Chicago and wrote columns for the *New York Age* about lynching. She noted the dates and people who were innocent and had been lynched. Famed black reformer Frederick Douglass admired her courage to tell the shameful story of lynching in the South. Wells soon wrote a pamphlet, called *Southern Horrors*, about lynching. Her writing and her speeches drew widespread attention, and she was asked to speak around the United States and also in England and Scotland. It was unusual in those days for a single woman to travel to Europe, so Wells traveled with Dr. Georgia Patton, the first black female physician in Memphis. Her campaign to let the world know about lynching was working. The people of Britain were shocked. Wells helped form the British Anti-Lynching Committee.

When she returned home, she spoke during the Chicago Columbian Exposition. Wells's talks attracted many women. A club was even formed called the Ida B. Wells Club, and women gathered for discussions, lectures, and musical events.

Wells liked Chicago. She decided that this city would now be her home. But she would also continue to travel and give speeches. She returned to Britain in 1894 and was pleased that several British groups now actively condemned lynching. But it was back in the United States where she had to do more. When she returned to the U.S., she spoke to both black and white audiences. She became friends with women's rights advocate Susan B. Anthony and embraced that cause, too.

The Wells-Barnett family's home in Chicago

Once, when Anthony invited Wells to her house, Anthony's secretary refused to work for Wells because she was black. Anthony fired her immediately. Wells was proud of her friend's unwavering support.

But there were two areas in which they differed. Anthony believed that women's rights should be supported equally with black rights and resented that black men were granted the vote and not women. Anthony wouldn't invite Frederick Douglass to a meeting because she was afraid that southern women would be offended. Wells disagreed.

Frederick Douglass

And when Wells married Ferdinand Barnett, an attorney and newspaper publisher in 1895, Anthony worried that married life would take Wells away from the causes she believed in. Some blacks worried about that, too.

WELLS FIGHTS ON

Wells's friends shouldn't have worried. Wells didn't let marriage and children deter her from speaking up and writing about the causes that were important to her. Wells even kept her maiden name, an unusual step for women at that time. She now called herself Ida B. Wells-Barnett.

Wells also became more involved with the Ida B. Wells Clubs and started a new kind of school in those days—a kindergarten.

Ferdinand Barnett

Even when Wells had her own child, Charles, she continued to travel and speak at conferences and clubs. Sometimes she would take Charles with her. In 1897, when Wells had her second child, Herman, she took time off to spend more time with her children.

And then in 1898, a black postman was lynched in Lake City, South Carolina. A mob set his house on fire and killed the postman and his infant. Wells was outraged. She traveled to Washington, D.C., to speak to President William McKinley. The president treated her with respect and offered to help. But when the

Wells and her four children

Spanish–American War broke out, the president's attention was taken up with the war. There was less interest in her cause and in stopping lynchings.

President William McKinley

WE MUST UNITE

Wells believed it was crucial for blacks to unite and work together toward common goals. But coming together was hard. People had different agendas. Famed educator and political leader Booker T. Washington was part of one group in the National Afro-American Council. He believed that education was key, and he was less interested in political action. Wells had more radical ideas. She wanted political change. She felt that blacks would never receive fair treatment and justice until laws were changed. Some people called her a hothead. There were also rivalries and power struggles, which divided the group. The disagreements prevented people from working successfully together.

In 1901, Wells's daughter Ida was born, and in 1904, another daughter, Alfreda, was born. Wells's family was one of the first black families to move into a white neighborhood in Chicago, but the neighbors weren't pleased with their new neighbors. Sometimes Wells's boys got into fights with local white boys. Many of Wells's white neighbors shunned them. But despite that, Wells and her family enjoyed good times in their new home listening to music and inviting company for supper.

Booker T. Washington

RIOTS

In 1908, riots broke out in Springfield, Illinois. White mobs burned black houses and stores. Three blacks were lynched. It was clear that some whites wanted to drive blacks out of the city. Wells thought that blacks weren't fighting hard enough to stop the violence. She and a group of other residents started an organization that would eventually call itself the National Association for the Advancement of Colored People (the NAACP). Many whites who supported fairness for blacks also supported the NAACP.

NAACP logo

In the fall of 1909, there was another lynching in Cairo, Illinois. A homeless black man was arrested for a crime but never brought to trial. A mob found him and lynched him instead. Wells took the train to Cairo to find out what happened. She discovered that the sheriff had not protected the black man. Wells spoke up in the courtroom in Cairo and was so impressive that when she was finished, every white man in the courtroom shook her hand. The governor of Illinois supported her, too. He promised that there would be no more lynchings in his state, and there weren't.

Wells also continued to fight for women's rights. In March 1913, some white women in the suffrage movement asked the black women to march separately in Washington. Wells refused. Instead, she joined an Illinois group who welcomed blacks. Wells marched side-by-side with them at the parade.

Ida B. Wells

After World War I, Wells continued to speak out. When she and her family moved into a prosperous neighborhood in Chicago, some black families' homes in the area were bombed. In 1919, riots broke out, and tensions arose between blacks and whites. More than five hundred people were injured in the violence that followed.

Wells continued to speak up wherever there was injustice against blacks or women. She even ran for state senator of Illinois in 1930. At the time, she was in the middle of writing her autobiography. She wanted to tell her story as only she could tell it.

Ida B. Wells died on March 25, 1931, of kidney failure. Her home in Chicago is a national historical landmark, and in 1990, the U.S. postal service issued a stamp in her honor.

ALICE PAUL

"Mr. President, how long must women wait to get their liberty? Let us have the rights we deserve."

ALICE PAUL fought long and hard to pass the Nineteenth Amendment to the U.S. Constitution, granting women the right to vote. She endured jail, hunger strikes, and force-feeding for the cause she believed in. The Nineteenth Amendment was passed in 1920. Paul continued to work toward equal opportunity for women for the rest of her life.

EARLY YEARS

Alice Paul was born in Mount Laurel, New Jersey, on January 11, 1885. Her family was made up of devout Quakers, who traced their ancestry back to William Penn, founder of Pennsylvania. Like most Quakers, the Pauls were against war and believed in fairness and equality. They felt that everyone, including women, should have a voice in discussions and decisions.

Paul's father, William, was a successful businessman. Paul's mother, Tacie, was a member of the National American Woman Suffrage Association (**NAWSA**) and attended meetings supporting equal rights and the vote for women. Sometimes her mother even took Alice along to meetings.

The Pauls were affluent, but they didn't flaunt their success. They owned a large farm, called Paulsdale, and felt that people should live simply and close to nature. They were proud of Alice, their eldest child. She was smart and capable from the time she was a young girl. Her father often said, "If you want something hard and disagreeable done, I bank on Alice to do it."

Paul attended the Friends School and graduated first in her class in 1901. At sixteen, she began studies at Swarthmore College, a coeducational school her grandfather had founded in 1864. It was also where her mother had been

Swarthmore College

a student. Going away to school was exciting. Paul liked the camaraderie of her fellow students. She liked being able to wear colorful clothes instead of the drab, severe clothes the Quakers favored. She liked being exposed to music and dance.

HELPING OUT

As a biology major, Paul was taught by some of the best female teachers of the time. But toward the end of her four years at Swarthmore, she decided to switch directions and pursue studies in social work, a newly recognized profession. Its focus was to support people in need. Paul decided that was just what she wanted to do—help improve people's lives. She was excited to get a scholarship after graduation, and set off for New York's Lower East Side. There, she'd work among immigrants, mostly from Europe, who flocked to the neighborhoods' crowded streets.

As soon as she arrived, she was astonished at how different the Lower East Side was from her home in rural New Jersey. The bustling streets were lined with pushcarts brimming with unfamiliar food. There was constant noise, and the air was thick with strange smells. People were poor, often sick, living in unsanitary conditions, and had little medical help or means to find better housing.

Paul threw herself into her work, but it was often unrewarding. There wasn't much she could do to really

Mulberry Street, New York City, circa 1900

make people's lives better. She told her mother, "You couldn't change the situation by social work." Without government assistance and new laws, a social worker had limited resources. After a year, Paul realized that she couldn't go on working this way, and social work wasn't for her. She decided to return to school and get a masters degree in sociology. When a Quaker group awarded her a scholarship to study in England, she accepted it.

SPEAKING UP

In England, Paul was busy with classes, volunteering at a settlement house, playing tennis, bicycling, and making new friends. And then one day, she attended a meeting that propelled her in a whole new direction.

Christabel Pankhurst

It was a talk by Christabel Pankhurst about equal rights for women, and it made a huge impression on Paul. Pankhurst was fearless and passionate. She and her mother, Emmeline Pankhurst, were at the forefront of the women's rights movement in England. Their motto was "Deeds, not words." Paul couldn't believe how these strong English women were met with jeers and protests. Paul was used to the quiet and agreeable manner in which Quakers held discussions. When she witnessed how the English audience treated Pankhurst, she felt sympathy and admiration for the cause of women's rights and the women who fought fearlessly for change.

Emmeline Pankhurst

On a clear June day in 1908, the English suffrage movement held one of the largest demonstrations that England had ever seen. Thirty trains carried women from seventy different towns to the capital. They marched, made speeches, and proclaimed, "Votes for Women." Watching the parade, Paul was impressed with the passion of the speakers and their courage. But even after that large demonstration, British Prime Minister Herbert Henry Asquith refused to alter his views or take any action in support of women's rights.

Paul knew that she wanted to become part of this powerful women's rights movement and began attending meetings. She was convinced that this was the way to make real changes in women's lives. If women had the vote, they could help make better laws.

Released prisoners demanding tha other women in prison be treated as political prisoners, no criminals.

Soon, Paul was also giving speeches and handing out newsletters in support of the women's rights cause. She was eager to help Pankhurst and their militant Women's Social and Political Union (WSPU). They were determined to force the prime minister out of office if he didn't listen to their demands for rights. The WSPU believed that polite requests, petitions, and reasonable discussions hadn't worked. It was time to be confrontational. They were even ready to hurl rocks at windows and disrupt elections to ensure that politicians paid attention. Their assertive actions brought them public attention and front-page headlines in the newspapers.

And Paul was right there in the middle of it all. She dressed as a cleaning lady to disrupt a meeting in Scotland. She heckled members of Parliament and climbed up on the roof to throw stones at the prime minister's window. She later claimed that she had personally broken forty-eight windows.

But despite her active involvement in WSPU meetings, Paul didn't neglect her studies. She was often the only woman and the only American in her classes. She impressed her professors with her hard work and keen intelligence. Soon she decided to take her studies beyond a master's degree and work toward a doctorate. Her family

Members of the WSPU on a horse-drawn bus covered with posters advertising their cause

Emmeline Pethick-Lawrence, a British suffrage leader, and Alice Paul

didn't approve of her plans. They thought it was time for Paul to come home. They refused to help her any longer with tuition or living expenses, but Paul was determined. She wanted to stay in England, continue her studies, and work for women's rights.

And if she couldn't get financial help from her family, she'd find a job. She soon found work in a rubber factory and boarded in a small, damp attic room. She also kept studying and fighting for the cause that had become so important to her.

JAILED

By the fall of 1910, Paul had been jailed three times for her activities supporting women's rights. She refused the money her mother offered to pay for fines and keep her out of prison. Like other suffragettes, Paul felt she'd been arrested on flimsy charges and was being treated like a common criminal. Suffragettes were searched and forced to wear uncomfortable clothing, sleep on plank beds, do endless demeaning chores, and eat miserable meals. Sometimes they were even thrown into solitary confinement.

Lucy Burns in prison

But to Paul and other militant suffragettes, being jailed was also a form of protest. Paul wrote her mother not to worry: "Other women are doing it. Why should not I?" And when Paul, like other suffragettes, went on a hunger strike and then were force-fed at the orders of the government, she coped—although she admitted later that it was torture. She hoped never to be force-fed again. Nevertheless, Paul's hunger strike hadn't gone unnoticed. It had even made headlines in the U.S.

By 1910, Paul decided to return home to the United States. She loved England, but she missed her family. After a rough Atlantic crossing, she stepped off the ship, greeted by her family and a few reporters. She was back, ready to continue her studies and her fight for women's rights.

THE FIGHT GOES ON!

Paul finished her doctoral dissertation in the U.S. and continued her activities in the women's rights movement. She gave speeches and interviews about her experiences in England and the importance of the women's rights movement. She believed that women had to pressure U.S. politicians if they were going to be granted the vote. She said, "The militant policy is bringing success . . . the agitation has brought England out of Her lethargy, and women of England are now talking of the time when they will vote, instead of the time when their children would vote, as was the custom a year or two back."

Now that there was a new president, Woodrow Wilson, in the White House, Paul wanted to make the case for women's rights strongly and directly to him. It wasn't going to be easy. Wilson was opposed to giving women the vote.

Paul and the NAWSA staged a huge parade on Pennsylvania Avenue to gain publicity for their cause. It would coincide with Wilson's inauguration in 1913. They turned the women's suffrage event into an elaborate pageant with people dressed up in costumes. Pageants were in fashion at the time and people flocked to see them. When male opponents began to attack the group, the police looked away. The parade and the cause of women's rights made national headlines.

Alice Paul, far left, in New York City

PRESIDENT WILSON

Paul and a group of other women from the suffrage movement met President Wilson in the White House for the first time in 1913. The women tried to persuade the president that granting women the vote fit into his ideals of democracy. He brushed them off, discounted their opinions, and said he was busy and needed more information. When the group came back to discuss the issues again, Wilson found other excuses to dismiss their arguments. Paul was now convinced that the only way the president would change his attitude was through pressure. She was determined to spearhead that pressure.

Paul and her colleagues in the NAWSA began staging more dramatic events to highlight their goals. A cross-country automobile caravan of women traveled from coast to coast to gather petitions that were delivered to Congress. During Wilson's 1916 State of the Union speech, the women unfurled a banner that read: "Mr. President, what will you do for woman suffrage?"

Paul used the skills she'd learned in the British suffrage movement to raise money and awareness. She opened her headquarters right across from the White House. She was adept at raising money and promoted a newspaper, *The Suffragist*. She sent women out to the streets of Washington, D.C., to sell their papers. She hired a cartoonist to portray

Paul, second from right, and suffragists picketing outside the Metropolitan Opera House

Wilson as a confused captain of a ship and a drowning man rescued by women. She encouraged women to stand up and speak out and not be afraid. She courted wealthy women, like Alva Vanderbilt Belmont, to help the cause by donating money. She spoke to classmates from Swarthmore and enlisted their help. She created an all-female advisory board of distinguished women. But no matter whom she brought to help the cause, Paul always maintained control of its direction.

A woman selling *The Suffragist* on the street

She was forceful and focused, and never took no for an answer.

A TENSE TIME

As time went on, Paul and the NAWSA increasingly disagreed about timing and tactics. The NAWSA leadership didn't like Paul's strong, direct approach with President Wilson. They supported the president and considered his party, the Democrats, allies. Paul believed that the only way

Paul at the National Woman's Party office

to make change was never to back down. She thought it was important to use every opportunity to keep the pressure on a reluctant and sometimes disdainful president. After all, Wilson had described women's suffrage as "this cause . . . for which you can afford to wait." Paul felt that women had waited too long already. They couldn't wait for the president to change his mind. They had to change it for him.

Tensions were so heated that Paul and her followers were tossed out of the NAWSA, and in 1916 formed the National Woman's Party (**NWP**). The NWP continued picketing the president even when the U.S. entered World War I. Throughout 1917, they stood outside at their posts near the

White House and stayed there despite rain, sleet, and snow. They picketed every day except Sunday.

To promote their cause, they used Wilson's own words about making the world safe for democracy. Their banner read: "We will fight for the things we have always held nearest our hearts, for Democracy, for the right of those who submit to authority to have a voice in their own government." They asked Wilson why he wasn't bringing democracy to American women. Didn't they deserve the right to help choose their own government just like citizens of any other country?

Suffragists at the 1920 Republican National Convention in Chicago

In June 1917, the NWP's banners were ripped. Some think it was done on the orders of the White House. Soon, a mob attacked the picketing women when they replaced their banners. The police looked on and did nothing to stop the mob. And when the women wouldn't budge despite the harassment, they were arrested on flimsy charges of "obstructing traffic." When they were jailed, they refused to pay the fines. Tossed into rat-infested prison cells, they staged hunger strikes and were brutally force-fed by prison guards.

The day the NWP protesters were arrested, Paul was home, sick with fatigue, digestive problems, and possibly Bright's disease, a disease that had killed President Wilson's first wife. But luckily Paul recovered. She didn't have Bright's disease, and she was soon back on the picket lines. On October 20, 1917, Paul was arrested and sentenced to seven months in jail. Despite the threat of jail, more women picketed and more were arrested. Soon the jails were full of women

Drawing showing a woman being force-fed in prison

whose only action was to picket. As more women poured into the jail, the guards decided they didn't want Paul to influence them, so they isolated her.

When news filtered out about the brutal treatment of the women in jail, the public was outraged. There was a demand for their immediate release. More people embraced the fight for women's rights, and sympathy for the cause grew.

By November 28, the suffragists were released. Some of the women were sick. Some were close to a total collapse. The judge's excuse for releasing the women was that "further imprisonment might be dangerous to their health." It was terrible being jailed, but the women had not given in despite horrific conditions. The battle for women's rights had not been won yet.

Alice Paul left prison thinner, but more determined than ever. She was convinced that what they had done and how they'd refused to budge from their position would change everything.

THE NINETEENTH AMENDMENT

There was now more general support for granting women the vote. Even President Woodrow Wilson knew it was time to change his attitude. Wilson called his sudden support a "war measure" and in 1919, after continued lobbying, picketing, and pressure, Congress finally passed the Nineteenth Amendment. They called it the Susan B. Anthony Amendment.

What was needed now was **ratification** from three-fourths of the states. Paul knew it was going to be hard to secure all the needed states to ratify. There were different state governments with opposing opinions and contradictory agendas. Paul knew that most of the southern states, like Georgia and Alabama, would vote no to the amendment, and they did. It was touch and go with some other states, like New Jersey and Oklahoma. But they finally supported the amendment.

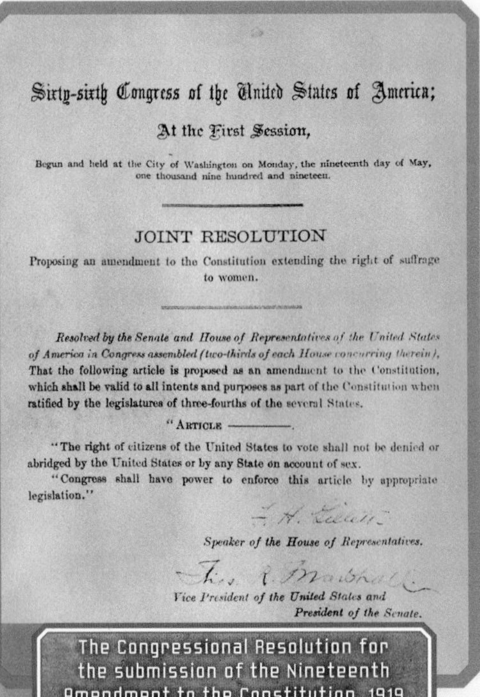

Sixty-sixth Congress of the United States of America;

At the First Session,

Begun and held at the City of Washington on Monday, the nineteenth day of May, one thousand nine hundred and nineteen.

JOINT RESOLUTION

Proposing an amendment to the Constitution extending the right of suffrage to women.

Resolved by the Senate and House of Representatives of the United States of America in Congress assembled (two-thirds of each House concurring therein), That the following article is proposed as an amendment to the Constitution, which shall be valid to all intents and purposes as part of the Constitution when ratified by the legislatures of three-fourths of the several States.

"ARTICLE ———.

"The right of citizens of the United States to vote shall not be denied or abridged by the United States or by any State on account of sex.

"Congress shall have power to enforce this article by appropriate legislation."

Speaker of the House of Representatives.

Vice President of the United States and President of the Senate.

The Congressional Resolution for the submission of the Nineteenth Amendment to the Constitution, 1919

In the end, it all came down to Tennessee. The majority of the state legislature had to ratify the Nineteenth Amendment, and then it would become law. For a while, it looked hopeless. At the last minute, the youngest member of the state senate, twenty-four-year-old Harry Burn who was about to vote no, received a letter from his mother. It read: "Hurrah and vote for suffrage and don't keep them in doubt." Burn voted yes. With his vote, the Nineteenth Amendment was ratified after a seventy-two-year struggle.

Harry Burn, a Tennessee state senator

It was a victory and a wonderful moment, but Paul knew that the fight for equal rights wasn't over. There was much more work to be done to make sure that women were treated equally by law and paid an equal wage for equal work.

LATER YEARS

In 1923, on the seventy-fifth anniversary of the Seneca Falls convention, which had started the women's rights movement, led by Paul's heroes—Elizabeth Cady Stanton and Susan B. Anthony—Paul announced that she would be working toward the ratification of the Equal Rights Amendment (ERA). This amendment called for "equal rights throughout the United States."

In 1943, it was named the Alice Paul Amendment. As Paul continued to push for the ERA, she also earned

Alice Paul and fellow suffragists at work

three law degrees. She traveled around the world advocating for women's rights. She worked to make sure the United Nations' charter included a commission on the status of women. She led a group that added a sexual discrimination clause into the Civil Rights Act of 1964. She was tireless, relentless, and always focused on her goals.

The women's movement picked up steam again in the 1960s. Once again, women marched and demanded equal pay and fairer laws. In 1972, the United States Congress finally passed the ERA. But to date, not enough states have ratified it to pass the amendment.

Alice Paul died at the age of ninety-two in 1977. Paul has been honored with stamps in the United States and Great Britain, and buildings at Swarthmore College and Montclair State University have been named in her honor. But perhaps her greatest legacy is the Nineteenth Amendment, which finally gave women a voice in their own destiny.

Paul admiring Lucretia Mott's bust in the Sewall-Belmont Museum in Washington, D.C.

ROSA PARKS

"I knew someone had to take the first step and I made up my mind not to move."

ROSA PARKS not only spoke up against discrimination, she acted on it. In 1955, she refused to sit at the back of a bus, as blacks were forced to do in those days in the South. Her courageous action spurred on a movement for equal rights and equal opportunity.

EARLY YEARS

Rosa Louise McCauley was born in Tuskegee, Alabama, on February 4, 1913. It was a time when blacks were treated as second-class citizens in southern states like Alabama. They were forced to eat in separate restaurants, sit at the back of city buses, live in separate neighborhoods, and even drink out of different water fountains.

Parks's grandfather, Sylvester Edwards, the son of a white plantation owner and his black housekeeper, never forgot the abusive way he was treated as a child. He was often hungry and had to go barefoot. He told Parks that she should never put up with being mistreated from anyone.

Parks's mother, Leona Edwards, believed that getting a good education, working hard, and being careful with money were important to succeed in life, no matter what obstacles you face. Leona was a teacher who'd attended an all-black university in Selma, Alabama.

Parks's father, James, was a carpenter who traveled for work and was hardly ever home. After Parks's brother, Sylvester, was born, her mother decided that Parks and Sylvester should live with their grandparents on their farm in Pine Level, Alabama. Leona would spend the week near her teaching job and return to her family on the weekend. By then Parks's parents had separated, and Parks rarely saw her father.

The children worked hard helping their grandparents pick walnuts, peaches, apples, and pecans on the farm, but they also had fun fishing in the nearby creek, exploring the woods, and hearing their grandparent's tell stories about their lives. To make ends meet, everyone in the family picked cotton on a local plantation. It was hot, backbreaking work, but they needed the money. Although she could only go to school five or six months a year, Parks was an avid reader and a good student.

She also stood up for herself. When she was about ten, a white boy threatened to beat her up with his fists. Parks told him she'd throw a brick at him if he tried, and he backed off.

African American women picking cotton

GROWING UP

After World War I ended in 1918, the Ku Klux Klan, a white organization that terrorized and often murdered innocent blacks, increased their activities in the South. Blacks never knew when or where the Klan would strike next. Parks remembered seeing her grandfather sitting with a gun in his lap ready to defend his family in case the Klan showed up. Luckily, they never did. But the fear that they might was always present.

There were other changes after the war, too. The small school in Pine Level that the children attended closed down. Leona sent Parks to live with relatives in Montgomery to continue her education. Montgomery was a big, bustling city in Alabama, and for the first time in her life, Parks really experienced the Jim Crow laws. These laws were formal ways of **segregating** blacks and whites. Pine Level was too small to have many separate facilities, but Montgomery was full of them. As a black person, you were forced to eat in different restaurants and attend different schools and churches. You even had to be buried in a separate cemetery.

One day, Parks walked through a white neighborhood on her way to school and was shoved by a white boy zipping past her on roller skates. Parks pushed him back. The boy's mother threatened to toss Parks in jail. Parks told her mother that the boy had pushed her first, but Parks's mother knew that didn't matter in a segregated society, when all the power was in the hands of whites. She soon moved Parks to another family member's home in a different part of Montgomery. Leona didn't want her daughter to walk to school past a white neighborhood again.

There were no public high schools that blacks could attend at the time, but Leona was determined that Parks go to high school. She saved money and sent her to the Montgomery Industrial School for Girls, a private school, which many called Miss White's School for Girls. Miss White, a white abolitionist teacher from Massachusetts,

Rosa Parks (right) sitting on a bus in 1955

founded the school to give black girls an opportunity to study and learn new skills. Parks liked school. She said, “We were taught to be ambitious and to believe that we could do what we wanted in life.”

While at Miss White’s, Parks had her tonsils removed after suffering for years from colds and sore throats. She even had difficulty swallowing. Feeling better was a great relief, but Parks was disappointed to learn that she couldn’t finish her studies at Miss White’s. After years of struggle, Miss White closed her school. She was tired of being harassed by the white community for running a school for blacks. Luckily, a junior high had just opened for black students, and Parks went there until ninth grade. Then she attended the laboratory school at Alabama State Teacher’s College High School.

Parks was determined to earn a high school degree, but when her grandmother and her mother took sick, she returned home to care for them and help out at the farm. She was only sixteen.

RAYMOND PARKS

Two years after Rosa returned to Pine Level, she met Raymond Parks. He was ten years older than Rosa. His father was white and his mother was black. His father had abandoned the family, and Raymond had a hard time

Rosa Parks in 1955

growing up as a mixed-race child. He was even excluded from school, so his mother taught him at home. When he met Rosa, he was working as a barber.

Rosa liked Raymond immediately. He was kind, well-read, and believed, as she did, that the unfair and discriminatory laws in the United States toward blacks had to be changed. Rosa married Raymond and he encouraged her to finish high school at the laboratory school. But even after obtaining a high school degree, Rosa found few opportunities for work. To make matters worse, the Great Depression had hit the U.S. Jobs were scarce for everyone, but especially for blacks.

Meanwhile, Raymond, who was one of the first members of the NAACP (the National Association for the Advancement of Colored People), was organizing a legal defense for nine black boys, called the Scottsboro Boys, who were convicted of rape and sentenced to death. The case was controversial, and it was dangerous to attend NAACP meetings. Two of

Raymond's colleagues had been killed by the local police. Although Rosa believed in the work Raymond was doing, she worried about his safety. It was tense and scary to realize he faced danger every day.

The Scottsboro case bounced back and forth between the U.S. Supreme Court and the Alabama Court. In the end, four of the boys were released, and the others were given long prison terms, even though it was clear that the white women who'd accused them of rape had lied.

PARKS AND THE VOTE

During World War II, Parks took a secretarial job at the Maxwell Air Force Base. It was wonderful to work in an integrated environment. For the first time in her life, Parks could sit near whites, eat with whites, and be treated as an equal. She said, "Maxwell opened my eyes up."

She joined the NAACP because she was impressed that their efforts had helped persuade Roosevelt to integrate the army. But while Parks was joining the NAACP, Raymond had resigned from the organization. He felt that the NAACP ignored the ideas of blue-collar workers like himself.

For twelve years, Parks served as the volunteer secretary for the NAACP in Montgomery. She collected information

SPORTS ★ FINAL

DAILY NEWS

NEW YORK'S HOMETOWN NEWSPAPER

1913-2005

ROSA PARKS

7053

PAGES 2-3

Front page of *Daily News* commemorating Parks's death

about crimes against blacks, helped publicize cases, and organized legal defenses. She was involved in combating the Jim Crow laws. She worked toward desegregating buses and tried to help blacks register to vote.

As she studied voting documents, she was shocked to learn that in Montgomery, with a black population of fifty thousand people, only thirty-one people were registered to vote. She realized that the registration office was open for only a few hours, and blacks, unlike whites, had to take a test—a long, complicated questionnaire with detailed questions about the U.S. Constitution. That made it hard for blacks to register, let alone vote. And then there was the poll tax, a hefty fee for a poor person. No wonder few blacks voted.

Parks was determined to test out the process herself. She knew that voting was one of the key ways to give blacks a voice in the government and work to change unfair laws. She filled out the registration forms, took the test, and waited. She was sure she'd passed, but to her dismay, she

Parks works as a seamstress after the Montgomery bus boycott, 1956

was denied registration. She tried again, and again she was denied. She tried again, and on her third try, her registration was accepted. Now all she had to do was pay the poll tax. She didn't earn much money, but this was so important that she decided to pay the tax despite the financial hardship. And then, Rosa Parks voted for the first time.

CHANGING TIMES

During World War II, many black soldiers were treated with dignity and respect when they helped liberate Europe. It was a shock to return to the United States

Parks at the 1963 Freedom March in Washington, D.C.

and be mistreated by whites in the South again. Parks's brother, Sylvester, was so outraged when he returned home from the war, he moved his family to Detroit, Michigan. He wanted Rosa and Raymond to move to Detroit, too. When Parks visited Detroit, she was amazed at the integrated buses, but she was uncomfortable by the race riots in the city. She decided to stay in Alabama and continue to work toward equality from her home in the South.

Then in 1954, the Supreme Court passed a law that would dramatically affect civil rights in the United States. In *Brown v. Board of Education*, the court ruled in favor of Oliver Brown from Kansas, who'd protested that his seven-year-old daughter had been prevented from attending an all-white school near her home. Instead, she had to travel to a black school. Brown and other black families who joined the case hoped that the "separate but equal" discriminatory ruling that allowed states to segregate schools would finally be overturned. At first, the local courts ruled against Brown, but when the case was heard in the Supreme Court, the justices said that the "separate but equal" rule in the South was unconstitutional. It was a huge step in ending discrimination.

A DAY TO REMEMBER

Parks continued to volunteer at the NAACP. She also tailored clothes to support her family. Her mother was sick, and Raymond wasn't well, either.

Then, in the early 1950s, Parks met Virginia Durr, a remarkable white socialite and activist. Virginia Durr had gone to college, which was unusual for a southern woman of her time. She'd helped progressive black educator Mary

Nettie Hunt explains to her daughter that segregation in public schools is now unconstitutional

McLeod Bethune fight to abolish poll taxes and change Jim Crow laws. When Parks and Durr became friends, Durr recommended Parks for a ten-day training workshop on integrating public schools at the Highlander Folk School in Tennessee. The Highlander, founded by Myles Horton, a champion of civil liberties, helped people fight for workers' rights and promote racial equality. Parks loved her time there. It felt wonderful to be in a place where it didn't matter if you were black or white. Everyone worked toward a common goal. Parks said that at Highlander, "We forgot about what color anybody was."

Emmett Till

On her return home that summer, Parks and many others in the United States were shocked at the brutal torture and killing of a young black boy named Emmett Till by two white men. People were even more enraged when an all-white jury in Mississippi found the murderers not guilty. It was clear there was still a long struggle ahead to make the courts rule in a fair and unprejudiced way, especially in the South. In August, Parks met a young black preacher named Martin Luther King, Jr., who was also involved in the fight for equality. She was impressed with his eloquence and determination to change how blacks were treated in the United States.

Then, on December 1, 1955, Parks took action, changing her life and the lives of many other blacks. After being a part of the NAACP for over a decade, Parks knew a great deal about segregationist issues and civil rights organizing. Her training in the NAACP prepared her for this very moment. As she stepped onto the bus she took every day on

Rosa Parks stepping onto bus

her way home from work, she sat down in the first row of the "colored" seats. These seats were designated for black people, unless white people needed them. Suddenly, she looked up and noticed that the bus driver, James Blake, was the same man who'd almost thrown her off a bus years before when she protested where she was forced to sit. As the bus filled up with whites, Blake again ordered the blacks to vacate their seats in the front rows. A few blacks beside Parks moved, but Parks wouldn't. Blake confronted her:

Parks after being arrested

"Are you going to stand up?" he barked.

"No," she replied.

"Then I'm going to have you arrested," said Blake.

"You may do that," said Parks.

And he did.

At the police station, Parks asked for a drink of water. She was refused. "It's for whites only," she was told. When she asked to make a phone call, she was refused again. Then she was fingerprinted and put behind bars.

THE CIVIL RIGHTS MOVEMENT

In jail, one of the women in a cell offered Parks some water from her own cup. Parks was grateful, and the woman told Parks her story. She'd been abused by a boyfriend, and after threatening him, had been jailed. The woman was desperate to tell her family what happened, but she wasn't allowed to contact them. Parks promised that when she was released, she'd call the woman's brothers.

When Rosa was finally able to call Raymond, he raced down to the jail. A friend gave him $100 to bail Rosa out of jail. The Parks family didn't have enough money themselves.

By the time Parks was released, word about what had happened on the Montgomery bus had spread. The black community asked Parks if she'd be willing to lead a class-action suit to challenge Montgomery's Jim Crow laws. She knew that it could be dangerous. She knew that some whites would harass her. She worried about losing her job. But Parks also knew that someone had to take the risk. This was important. "I was determined to achieve the total freedom that our history lessons taught us we were entitled to," she later explained. It was also important to keep her promise to her cellmate. Parks called the young woman's family as she'd promised.

Parks's decision to take action sparked a chain reaction in the Montgomery black community. There was a call for a black boycott of the Montgomery buses. At first, even activists like Martin Luther King, Jr., were reluctant to support a boycott, but Parks's words helped convince everyone. She explained how humiliated she felt being sent to the back of the bus. Soon, all the black ministers agreed to support the boycott. The word was out! Blacks would not take the bus. They would walk to work. The black community was united.

Martin Luther King, Jr., outlining boycott strategies to his organizers in 1956

Reverand Abernathy escorts Mrs. King and Parks at a memorial procession for Martin Luther King, Jr., in 1968

When Parks's trial finally took place, it was a sham. The only witnesses were bus driver James Blake and two white women. Parks was found guilty and ordered to pay a $14 fine. Her defense lawyer said he would appeal the verdict to a higher court, and the black community continued its boycott of the buses. The bus company refused to change its policies, and the boycott kept going. On January 7, 1956, Parks lost her job. One week later Raymond quit his job as the barber at the Maxwell Air Force Base in protest. His boss had declared that anyone discussing the boycott would be fired.

Parks bein finger-printed after bein arrested

boycott continued, it gained national and international attention. There were heightened tensions between the black and white communities in Montgomery. Parks received threatening phone calls. The white community indicted black leaders, including Parks Parks, for violating an old law that made boycotts illegal.

When a picture of Parks being fingerprinted was published on the front page of the *New York Times*, her fame spread. She was asked to speak at church rallies and meetings. She met Eleanor Roosevelt, wife of the former president, who wrote about her in her column, “My Day.”

On November 13, 1956, the Supreme Court ruled that bus segregation was unconstitutional. The bus boycott had lasted 381 days. Parks's refusal to change seats on a bus had made a difference.

LATER YEARS

Parks continued to speak up against unfair laws. But there was so much hostility toward her from the white community in Montgomery that she decided to finally move to Detroit. She also knew she would never find work in Montgomery again. In Detroit, she found work in a sewing factory and continued being active in the civil rights movement. She

Parks on a desegregated bus

Parks and Vice President Al Gore with he Congressiona Gold Medal

marched with Martin Luther King, Jr., to support President John F. Kennedy's Civil Rights Bill in 1963.

In 1964, President Lyndon B. Johnson passed the Civil Rights Act. Black candidates started entering politics and Parks worked for one of them—John Conyers—until she retired in 1988. By then she'd lost her mother, brother, and husband to cancer. In her last years, she was involved with the Parks and Raymond Parks Institute for Self

Development. It offered programs to help young people pursue their education.

Rosa Parks died on October 24, 2005. She was ninety-two. More than four thousand people attended her funeral. She was honored for her courage and as a key figure in changing attitudes and laws in the United States.

CONCLUSION

American women helped settle the first thirteen colonies, stood side by side with men in the fight for independence, and traveled westward under dangerous conditions to establish new communities. Yet despite all this, it took seventy-five years for women in the U.S. to be granted the right to vote, own property, or have a real say in their lives and future.

In the mid-1800s, Susan B. Anthony and Elizabeth Cady Stanton helped lead a movement for women's rights. Both grew up in affluent families where education was valued and fairness was respected. Both admired their fathers and wanted to make them proud. Both were eager to attend college but couldn't because, in their day, colleges refused to admit women.

For years, Anthony and Stanton worked tirelessly, often together, to promote equality for women. Although they had different strengths and temperaments, and sometimes disagreed, they never lost sight of their goal—ensuring that women were treated fairly and granted the vote.

Their courage and persistence inspired and energized generations of women who followed them, including Jane Addams, Ida B. Wells, Alice Paul, and Rosa Parks. These women admired how Anthony and Stanton promoted the cause of women's rights through nonviolent means, such as petitions, speeches, and protests. They were determined to continue the fight for fairness and equality despite continued opposition.

Anthony's and Stanton's efforts to ensure that universities accept women students impacted Alice Paul's and Jane Addams's lives. Paul not only acquired a BA, but several law degrees as well. Jane Addams, who was eventually awarded the Nobel Peace Prize for her work, attended college and was admitted to medical school.

Although Anthony and Stanton didn't live to see the Nineteenth Amendment finally pass in 1920, without their pioneering work it might never have happened. And without the tenacity of Paul, the amendment might not have overcome the continued and often fierce resistance of politicians, including President Wilson, to finally become law.

Determination, tenacity, and a belief in nonviolence defined the actions of civil rights leaders like Wells and Parks, too. They refused to allow a prejudiced and discriminatory society to continue to impose unfair laws on blacks. They never wavered in their position despite criticism, personal threats, and even being jailed.

The courage and perseverance of all six of these remarkable women changed their lives and the lives of all who came after them.

TIMELINE

- **1787:** U.S. Constitution is adopted, and each state can define their voting rights
- **1815:** Elizabeth Cady Stanton is born (née Elizabeth Cady)
- **1820:** Susan B. Anthony is born
- **1848:** Stanton, Lucretia Mott, and others draw up a declaration of women's rights
- **1852:** *Uncle Tom's Cabin* is published
- **1860:** Jane Addams is born
- **1860:** Abraham Lincoln is elected president of the United States
- **1861:** American Civil War begins
- **1862:** Ida B. Wells is born
- **1863:** Emancipation Proclamation issued by President Lincoln
- **1865:** American Civil War ends
- **1865:** Thirteenth Amendment is passed, which frees all slaves
- **1868:** Fourteenth Amendment is passed, granting citizenship to recently freed slaves
- **1869:** Anthony and Stanton form the National Woman Suffrage Association
- **1870:** Fifteenth Amendment is passed, giving black men the right to vote

- **1872:** Anthony registers to vote and is taken to court
- **1885:** Alice Paul is born
- **1888:** Anthony founds the International Council of Women to push for women's rights in other countries
- **1889:** Addams and Ellen Starr create Hull-House
- **1902:** Addams publishes her first book, *Democracy and Social Ethics*
- **1902:** Elizabeth Cady Stanton dies
- **1906:** Susan B. Anthony dies
- **1909:** Addams and Wells help found the NAACP
- **1912:** Woodrow Wilson is elected president of the United States
- **1913:** Rosa Parks is born (née Rosa McCauley)
- **1914:** World War I begins
- **1916:** Paul and her followers are ejected from the NAWSA and form the National Woman's Party
- **1918:** World War I ends
- **1920:** Nineteenth Amendment is passed, giving women the right to vote
- **1930:** Wells runs for state senator
- **1931:** Addams is the first woman to be awarded the Nobel Peace Prize
- **1931:** Ida B. Wells dies

- **1935:** Jane Addams dies
- **1939:** World War II begins
- **1945:** World War II ends
- **1954:** Supreme Court rules in favor of Oliver Brown in the *Brown v. Board of Education* case
- **1955:** Emmett Till is brutally murdered by two white men
- **1955:** Parks refuses to move to the back of a bus in Alabama
- **1956:** Supreme Court rules that bus segregation is unconstitutional
- **1964:** President Lyndon B. Johnson signs the Civil Rights Act
- **1964:** Paul pushes to have a sexual discrimination clause added to the Civil Rights Act
- **1972:** Congress passes the Equal Rights Amendment (to date, not enough states have ratified it to pass the amendment)
- **1977:** Alice Paul dies
- **2005:** Rosa Parks dies

Abolitionist: a person advocating for the liberation of slaves before the Civil War

Amendment: a change or addition that is made to a law or legal document

Anarchist: a person who doesn't believe in the role of government

Bloomers: loose-fitting knee-length pants worn under dresses that allowed easy, comfortable movement for women

Emancipation: the freedom of a person or group from slavery

Jim Crow laws: a set of laws first enacted in 1876, permitting the unfair treatment of blacks in the South

Ku Klux Klan: a secretive white organization that practiced racism against non-white groups of people

Lynching: the brutal killing of a person by hanging, specifically used on blacks in the South during the Jim Crow era

NAACP: the National Association for the Advancement of Colored People, a group founded in 1909 to promote the improvement of conditions for blacks in America

NAWSA: the National American Woman Suffrage Association, a group founded in 1890 to push equal rights and the vote for women

NWP: the National Woman's Party, a group formed in 1916 to continue fighting for women's right to vote

Pacifist: a person who believes very strongly that war and violence are wrong, and who refuses to fight or to enter the armed forces

Quaker: a member of the Religious Society of Friends, a religion which opposes war, promotes simple living styles, and upholds the equality of men and women

Ratification: an official agreement or approval

Reformer: a person who supports change in something so that it is corrected or improved

Segregation: the act or practice of keeping people or groups apart

Settlement house: a communal home providing shelter and food for the poor

Suffrage: the right to vote

Sweatshops: workshops where people worked for little pay in unfavorable conditions

BOOKS

Adler, David. *A Picture Book of Rosa Parks.* New York: Holiday House, 1995.

Ashby, Ruth. *Rosa Parks: Freedom Rider.* New York: Sterling, 2008.

Baker, Jean H. *Sisters: The Lives of America's Suffragists.* New York: Hill and Wang, 2006.

Faber, Doris. *Oh, Lizzie!: The Life of Elizabeth Cady Stanton.* New York: Lothrop, Lee & Shepard Company, 1972.

Fritz, Jean. *You Want Women to Vote, Lizzie Stanton?.* New York: G. P. Putnam's Sons, 1995.

Ginzberg, Lori D. *Elizabeth Cady Stanton: An American Life.* New York: Hill and Wang, 2009.

Hull, Mary, Gloria Blakely, and Heather Lehr Wagner. *Rosa Parks: Civil Rights Leader.* Philadelphia: Chelsea House, 2004.

Knight, Louise W. *Jane Addams: Spirit in Action.* New York: W. W. Norton & Company, 2010.

Mitchard, Jacquelyn. *Jane Addams: Pioneer in Social Reform and Activist for World Peace.* Milwaukee, Wisconsin: Gareth Stevens Children's Books, 1991.

Myers, Walter Dean. *Ida B. Wells: Let the Truth Be Told.* New York: Harper Collins, 2008.

Schraff, Anne. *Rosa Parks: "Tired of Giving In."* Berkeley Heights, New Jersey: Enslow Publishers, 2005.

Walton, Mary. *A Woman's Crusade: Alice Paul and the Battle for the Ballot.* New York: Palgrave Macmillan, 2010.

Ward, Geoffrey C. and Ken Burns. *Not for Ourselves Alone: The Story of Elizabeth Cady Stanton and Susan B. Anthony.* New York: Alfred A. Knopf, 1999.

Welch, Catherine. *Ida B. Wells-Barnett: Powerhouse with a Pen.* Minneapolis, Minnesota: Carolrhoda Books, 2000.

Wheeler, Jill C. *Rosa Parks.* Minneapolis, Minnesota: Abdo Pub. Co., 2002.

WEBSITES

http://www.alicepaul.org

http://www.answers.com/topic/ida-b-wells

http://www.digitalhistory.uh.edu

http://ecssba.rutgers.edu/

http://www.grandtimes.com/rosa.html

http://www.nytimes.com/learning/general/onthisday/bday/0906.html

http://www.rochester.edu/sba/suffragetimeline.html

http://rosaparks.org/

https://sites.google.com/a/umn.edu/historpedia/home/individual-people/alice-paul-equal-rights-spr10

http://www.spartacus.schoolnet.co.uk/FWWwells.htm

http://www.susanbanthonyhouse.org/her-story/biography.php

http://www.webster.edu/~woolflm/janeadams.html

http://www.winningthevote.org/sbanthony.html

http://www.womenshistory.about.com/od/stantonelizabeth/a/stanton.htm

INDEX

ALSO AVAILABLE

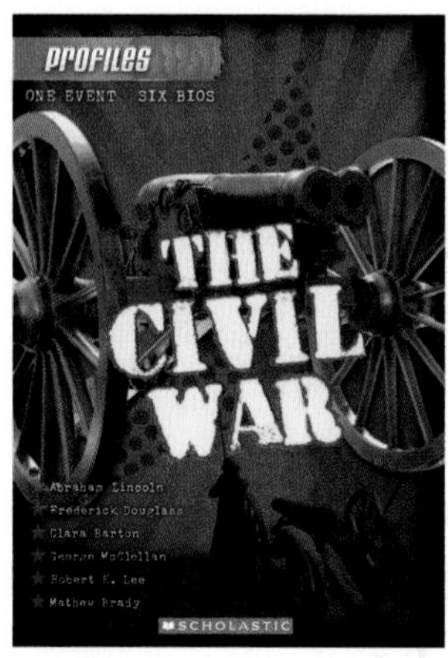

PROFILES: THE CIVIL WAR
978-0-545-23756-7

PROFILES: WORLD WAR II
978-0-545-31655-2

PROFILES: TECH TITANS
978-0-545-36577-2